7-Step System

CLIENT GETTING P.L.A.N.

How to Get All the Clients You Can Handle Without Cold Calling or Spending a Dime on Marketing!

By Drew Laughlin

Client Getting P.L.A.N.

For more information on this book and for further assistance please visit:

ClientGettingPlan.com

Note to Readers

The information presented herein represents the view of the author as of the date of publication. Because of the rate with which conditions change, the author reserve the right to alter and update his opinion based on the new conditions. This book is for informational purposes only. While every attempt has been made to verify the information provided in this book, neither the authors nor their affiliates/partners assume any responsibility for errors, inaccuracies or omissions. You should be aware of any laws, which govern business transactions or other business practices in your country and state. Any reference to any person or business whether living or dead is purely coincidental.

Every effort has been made to accurately represent this product and its potential. Examples in these materials are not to be interpreted as a promise or guarantee of earnings. Earning potential is entirely dependent on the person using our product, ideas and techniques. We do not purport this as a "get rich scheme."

Your level of success in attaining the results claimed in our materials depends on the time you devote to the program; ideas and techniques mentioned your finances, knowledge and various skills. Since these factors differ according to individuals, we cannot guarantee your success or income level. Nor are we responsible for any of your actions.

IMPORTANT: THIS BOOK WILL NOT WIN ANY GRAMATICAL OR SPELLING AWARDS. IF YOU'RE THE TYPE OF PERSON THAT FOCUSES ON HOW WELL THE BOOK IS WRITTEN I MAY DISAPPOINT YOU. HOWEVER, IT IS ONE OF THE MOST POWERFUL WAYS TO GET TONS OF CLIENTS. IF YOU'RE THE TYPE OF PERSON THAT WILL FOCUS ON THE CONTENT AND PREFERS TO GET STRAIGHT TO THE POINT WITH NO FLUFF THEN I'M CONFIDENT YOU'LL LOVE THIS BOOK!! BUT IF YOU FEEL THE NEED TO EDIT IT THEN FEEL FREE TO SEND ME YOUR NOTES! ☺

Download Your Free Bonus

Since you're a super cool person for reading this book I want to give you a free bonus gift!

Simply go to the webpage below and download your free surprise.

ClientGettingPlan.com/bonus

Table of Contents

Introduction

About twice per year I survey my customer list of several thousand consultants and entrepreneurs and ask them what they need help with. What's holding them back. And how I can help them grow their business.

Inevitably the overwhelming answer is always something like, "How can I get more clients?"

They tell me how great their product or service is and how they can help people but they just can't seem to find enough of them.

When I ask them what they've done in the past to get more client the typical answers come up. I'm sure you can guess what they are.

- Building a website
- Sending emails
- Attending "Tips Groups" meetings
- Asking for referrals
- Maybe, just maybe they've run PPC (Pay-Per-Click) advertising

Here's why that stuff doesn't work.

Those activities are too passive in nature and they do not set you up as an authority or the go-to expert in your field. It's almost like begging for clients.

Traditional marketing methods have always been about you and your company. Have you done this – or at least seen or heard of this before? "We've been in business for 25 years." "We're locally owned." "We have 100% certified technicians." "We use the latest technology to get the best results." Bla, bla, bla.

All of those things I just listed are important to a point. However, if you're using them as your main marketing message and then doing passive activities in an attempt to get more clients you're in a muddy field with slick tires. You'll be spinning your wheels forever trying to get out.

The Marketing World Has Changed

In today's game of marketing and lead generation it is all about the customer and how you and your business can help them solve their problems.

It's about you bringing them value!

It's about you making it about your customer and not the other way around. The consultant, entrepreneur, independent businesses person - any business for that matter - who gives value first and actually helps their customer BEFORE asking for the business will win the race.

WRITE THIS DOWN:

When I bring value first I'll never have to sell again!

What I mean by that is by you giving value to your prospective client first and actually helping them instead of "hard selling" the sales process becomes easy. You will be viewed as the authority. As the go-to expert. And as someone who has your client's best interest at heart. You will become the natural choice in a crowed world of white noise and "me-too" competition.

Who This Book is For

If you're a small business consultant, entrepreneur, independent professional, service-based business or anyone else who is looking to attract more small businesses as clients then this is for you.

While this P.L.A.N. can work for professionals who call on businesses in faraway places it is best used in your local market. Why? Simply because the system that I'm about to reveal to you is best used in your local market. Yes, you can use webinars and that model is quite effective. However, as you keep reading, you'll see why it's best to start local and then move outward from there.

And if you do in fact keep reading I promise that I will teach you not only a proven system – we have case studies to show you – but one that you can learn very quickly and implement in 30-45 days to literally get all the clients you need and be able to turn it on or off whenever you want.

Now of course I cannot guarantee results. I don't know you and your skill set, desire to succeed or anything else that determines your outcomes.

But what I can promise are the exact steps to follow that has worked for me and many of my students to get all the clients we can handle.

How This Book Came About

The original goal I had for the Client Getting PLAN was simply an online training course. In fact, that is what I created first, and it is currently available now and still attracts new customers every day.

At that time, I never really thought about turning it into a book. And then it happened. One of those total "Doh!" moments.

You see, I actually help entrepreneurs, business owners and consultants publish their book to build credibility and authority in their market place.

And one of those clients asked me why the Client Getting PLAN wasn't a book.

Like I said, a total "DOH!" moment.

What I did was take the transcripts of those videos, edit them for better reading and then turn them into the book you're reading here.

Some people learn best by reading. Others learn best by watching video and doing the exercises as they follow along.

Now I can serve even more people!

Pretty cool, right?!

If you 're one of those people that prefer an online video training program, then feel free to check out our special offer here:

ClientGettingPlan.com/course

Never Worry About Getting Clients Again

Like I mentioned in the introduction the biggest concern from my customers has always been finding new clients and customers for their consulting practice or business service.

Let's be honest. In the age of the Internet and immediate gratification it's tougher than ever to find clients. Much less the right clients.

Why More Clients Isn't Always the Answer

What would you rather have? An endless supply of clients that are high maintenance, complain endlessly, are never satisfied, haggle on price every time you talk to them and hammer you and your people daily with meaningless support issues.

Or would you rather have clients that are easy to work with, pay on time, pay what they are supposed to and never haggle on price and give you rave reviews and offer referrals without you asking for them?

Of course, this is a loaded question and I can say with confidence that you would much rather have customers that come from the second group than the first.

But let me ask you this. Why is it that so many of us seem to have way more clients and customers from group number one than group number two?

Usually it's because we simply don't have enough clients so we take what we can get.

Imagine a world where you don't have to take what you can get. Imagine being able to choose the customers and clients you want to work with and being able to FIRE the ones you don't!

I am here to tell you that is possible. And it's not only possible its exactly what myself and my customers are able to do after they implement the Client Getting P.L.A.N.

It's Not All Roses and Rainbows

Back in the day when the Internet really started to gain momentum there were people selling products and programs on how easy it was to get customers and clients online.

They promised riches without work. They promised push button solutions while you could sit back and watch the money roll in. Clearly this wasn't and still isn't the case. Sure there are some fantastic products, programs and technology that help us do important things easier and better than ever before. But the fact remains getting clients isn't one of them. It takes work. It takes effort.

Being a consultant, entrepreneur and independent business professional means we are in the "people business". We are not in automated call messaging business or the email spamming business.

We need to be seen, be heard and be viewed as an expert. So we can build trust, credibility and ultimate loyalty with our clients.

The people that are willing to do the work – even though it is relatively easy and fun – will win out over the ones who continuously look for the short cut or the easy way out. Are you someone who is willing to do what it takes to grow your business and to help as many people as your business deserves?

Then let me tell you a quick story.

How I Discovered the P.L.A.N.

While I pride myself on not being a moron, I can't always say the things I've done were the smartest.

For example, when I started my consulting practice, I had no idea what I was doing. I thought to myself, "Just do what everyone else is doing and you'll be fine."

Big. Huge. Mistake.

Why? Because everyone was doing it wrong! They were marketing themselves with a bunch of generic platitudes, sending out mailers that had no meaning, no uniqueness and no call to action. It seemed like everyone was copying everyone else, but no one knew how to do it right.

And of course, I just modeled them. Because I thought, "if they're doing it and they keep doing it and every one of their competitors is doing it then that's what I should do." It makes sense if in fact it was the right thing to do. But it wasn't.

I started studying marketing, public speaking and sales. Then after a while I discovered something that changed my life forever. I discovered three simple things that started attracting clients like crazy!

The three things are...

Be Seen

One of the best ways to get clients is simply by being visible in your marketplace. If you're someone who thinks they can get all the clients, they want by sitting behind a computer. I'm sorry to tell you but you're wrong. Smart people know they need to be seen to build relationships and trust with their market.

Be Heard

Have an opinion! Don't be someone who simply goes with what everyone else is saying. It's impossible to please everyone. So, don't try.

When you have the guts to express your thoughts on a topic and own those thoughts and opinions people will be drawn towards you like never before. People love different, new and unique perspectives. Give it to them.

Be an Expert

We can't be all things to all people we serve. I know we all want to but we just can't. Instead of focusing on several different things – never really getting good at any of them – why not start out by becoming the go-to expert in one thing? Being viewed as an expert is the surest way to get clients coming to you instead of the other way around.

Instead of sitting behind my computer and waiting and hoping for someone to call me I knew that I needed to get out there if I really wanted to make it.

The Idea That Changed Everything

I thought to myself…

Why not partner with a business that already has the people I want as customers as their customers.

It just makes sense, right? Partner with someone who already has my target market as their customers. If I can get in front of them, provide them value, help them solve their problems then they would naturally come to me for further assistance and help in my area of expertise.

The Ideal Partner

But who would that ideal partner be?

Really it could be any one. Just as long as they already had the people I wanted - as their customers.

As I processed my theory and thought long and hard about it one class of business made the most sense.

What business was that? Banks.

Yes, banks. But why banks?

Let's think about it. As a consultant who calls on local small businesses and provides them products and services, what does every small business already have? They have some sort of business account at their local bank or credit union.

Banks literally have 100% of our target market as their customers already!

Let's recap quickly to ensure we're all on the same page. If you're a consultant or any kind of business professional that sells to and needs more local small businesses as clients, then banks pretty much have your clients – or who you want as clients – as their customers already.

At this moment in time this was just theory. I had not put it to the test yet. It made perfect sense – as I hope you'd agree – but would it work in the real world?

I did the next logical thing to test my theory. And as most people in the world, I have a couple friends that work at banks. Fortunately, they work at different banks in different cities so this would give me a good gauge as to the potential of this.

I gave my friends a call and explained how I wanted to help them provide additional value and services to their existing clientele. At that time, I wasn't sure exactly how I was going to do that but what I did find out is that they were desperate to find new ways to bring value to their clients. There's only so much they can do. So if something new comes along that does not interfere or jeopardize their current relationship with their clients they were pretty excited to listen.

The Big Idea

That's when it hit me!

Right there on the phone I asked my bank buddy, "What if I came to your location and delivered a lunch-and-learn presentation on a topic that will actually help your customers in some way?"

He replied without thinking twice, "That would be awesome! Our customers would love that and it would make us look good too. And it would be a great excuse to bring them into our location to continue to build the relationship. I love this idea!"

Then he asked, "What would your presentation be about?"

After a slight pause I answered, "Not sure. Let me think about a couple topics that I can run by you. But I will tell you this. The presentation will be value heavy. Meaning I will not sit up there and talk about me and my company. That would be a waste of their time. But what I will do is bring a solution to a pesky problem they're having. Then hopefully after they see I'm there to help and I'm not just there to pitch them they'll look to hire me or at least talk with me about how I can help them individually."

He told me that sounded great and looked forward to my follow up call. Which of course went great. In fact, nearly every bank I called – even people I didn't know – loved the idea and wanted to run lunch-and-learns (L&Ls) for their customers.

After nearly four months of implementing the details of what you're about to discover – the P.L.A.N. - I no longer have to worry about clients. I can turn this client-generating faucet on or off any time I want.

Many of my students have done the same. Whether it's Dino who conducted three L&Ls and recently told me he doesn't have to do them anymore because he has too many clients! Or it's Ope – who lives in Nigeria by the way – who on his first call to a bank secured fifty L&Ls with different bank locations throughout the country. The really cool thing is he also received a $50,000 Logistics Fee! That's right, $1,000 per branch for his travel expenses and other stuff that a Logistic Fee covers. That's all Ope's idea too. I think its genius!

Now I can't guarantee your results. I don't know you, your skill set, your desire and even if you'll follow the 7-step system. But what I will promise you is that I will give you every detail of what I did and what my other students have done to get their results.

Sound fair?

Great! Let's dive a little deeper into the P.L.A.N.

What Is the P.L.A.N.?

The PLAN is a proven method that helps you attract small businesses and show them why you are the best one to help them.

There is no cold calling. There is no prospecting. And in many cases, you can have others be the ones footing the bill for your marketing expenses and lunch!

What is the P.L.A.N.?

The "P.L.A.N" stands for:

- Presentation
- Lunch
- Audience
- Network

In short, the secret sauce of the Client Getting P.L.A.N. is all about giving a problem-solution focused **Presentation** over **Lunch** – commonly known as a Lunch and Learn (L&L) – in front of a targeted **Audience** where you **Network** with the attendees after the presentation is over to build relationships and close deals or next steps.

While this model is simple to understand there are key success factors that make it work like a faucet you can turn on and off whenever you need more clients.

For example:

- You can't just give any kind of presentation. You can only give client-focused presentations, NOT something that's focused on you.
- Why lunch? Because it's proven to be a perfect time to get decision makers out of their office and attend something useful.
- Who gets the audience? Not you! It's left to someone else. That's the beauty of this entire system. You'll leverage someone else who already has your ENTIRE target market as their customer base but aren't your competitor!

During the networking phase you won't be just some lame person doing the same lame networking stuff. You'll be viewed as the expert authority on a topic your audience needs help with. They'll come to you!

The PLAN is very simply, to give lunch-and-learn presentations at banks.

Do I Have to Use Banks?

A common question I get is, "Do I have to give my lunch-and-learns at banks?'

The one-word answer is, "No".

You do not have to give your L&Ls at banks. There are many alternatives you can use. We'll talk about these more later, but you can do them at Chamber of Commerce events, Association Meetings, SCORE or any place else that has your target market as their customers.

The reason the PLAN focuses on banks is because they offer a great service that's needed by many, and they provide that service to – depending on how big the city – thousands and thousands of small business customers.

While banks offer a valuable service to their customers, they have a tough time adding value to their clients. They can compete amongst each other with better rates and better customer service, but there's nowhere else for them to really go. Yet they still have that need. That need to provide their clients with something more, something of value. And they can do that by offering lunch-and-learn presentations.

What is a Lunch-and-Learn Presentation?

It's exactly what it sounds like. A lunch-and-learn presentation is a short presentation, usually given over lunch. It's short and straight to the point.

The bank is really just the portal to the small business customer. They have the customers; you have the information on how to help those customers. By giving a presentation to those customers, you become viewed as the expert in your field, the bank becomes the one that offers that something extra to their customers, and the customers benefit by having their problems solved. It truly is a win-win-win situation for everyone.

Attracting new customers this way is incredibly effective, and very valuable. It's done by focusing on one problem the client is having and offering a solution to that problem. One problem. One solution. Using a short and sweet presentation style is very important because you won't find a bank or a client that wants you to come in and listen to you talk about yourself.

Don't tell them what your business offers. Don't tell them what you can do for them. Don't tell them anything that doesn't offer value to them.

One of the biggest mistakes you can make is delivering a traditional, boring business presentation where you talk about you and your business and how great you are.

You know the drill. You say platitudes like, "We're the leader in our industry." "We're the best at this and that." "We've been in business for xx years."

Stuff that may be important to you but frankly information that no one else cares about. But don't worry. We're going to cover exactly what your presentation should be and how it should flow later on in this book.

Before we do that let's talk about how L&Ls benefit you.

How The P.L.A.N. Benefits You

Many consultants, entrepreneurs and independent professionals still don't believe that lunch-and-learn presentations can help them. And some are even a bit intimidated by them. They don't want to get up in front of people and speak.

They believe that if they start giving away the answers to their client's questions, they'll simply go out and get the job done themselves, and not hire a consultant to do it for them.

Fortunately, the people that believe this are usually 100% wrong.

Lunch-and-learn presentations don't only benefit the bank and the attendee; they also benefit you and your business.

The reason clients aren't going to run off with the answer once you've given it to them and do it themselves is because they don't have the time nor the desire to do it themselves. They're too busy operating and managing their own business. In most cases, they haven't even had time to properly analyze the problem to come up with possible solutions, let alone carry out the execution of them.

Once you give them that answer though, you'll begin establishing yourself as an expert in the field. And once you talk to them for half-an-hour or so about that solution, how it will help them, and the results they can expect to see, you'll establish yourself as not just the expert, but the go-to expert in your field. They'll know quite clearly that you're the one that knows how to help them, and they'll want you to be the one that does the work for them.

What's even better is that the next time they have a problem; you'll be the first person they go to for the solution and execution.

The second reason people talk themselves out of giving lunch-and-learn presentations is because they think they couldn't possibly ever stand up in front of a crowd of people and speak. Public speaking is after all; the number one fear people have.

But lunch-and-learn presentations should <u>not</u> be considered public speaking. At least not in the same way as something like a guest speaker talking to a group of people that don't know who she is or why she's speaking. Which happens a lot at various events.

As mentioned before, lunch-and-learn presentations are very short, quick to the point. They're only between 20 and 40-minutes, and you usually present to no more than 15-20 people at a time.

Even more important is every person in attendance is there to see you. They will have signed up for it and know exactly what the topic is. They are going there to learn from you – the expert.

It's also important to remember that you CAN convince them you're the expert in your field, because you are. You'll be speaking about a topic that you know inside and out, and that you've been dealing with every single day. You're not going to be mumbling about something that you've had to do a ton of research on and is written on the notes you're fumbling through.

You will know what you're talking about, and you'll feel comfortable doing it. This is part of what will help establish you as the expert in your field.

Another benefit to giving lunch-and-learn presentations at banks is because they will likely foot the bill. Think about it. They're bringing an expert in – free of charge to those attending the presentation – to help small business owners and managers solve problems in their business.

They'll have the meeting room available, so you won't have to rent the space; and in many cases, they'll even do all the advertising for the presentation. Whether its time spent on emails or money spent on postage, it will most likely be at the expense of the bank. Nowhere else can you get that kind of value for your marketing dollar!

The only expense you may have to pay for or help pay for is the actual lunch. When I first started doing this, I was nervous about asking the bank to pay for lunch. But I went outside my comfort zone and did it and what do you know? They agreed!

Did all of them agree to buy lunch? No. Some wanted to split the bill with me. A couple of them wanted me to bring lunch in. In the end, it all depends on the bank, your relationship with them and your willingness to ask them to buy it.

Hopefully by this point you can envision how this system works. Of course, you probably have some questions. I'm confident the rest of the book will answer them because I go into great detail on how to execute this 7-step system.

But first I want to cover a couple thoughts that may be going through your head.

Does This Sound Like You?

Chances are you can see how powerful this system can be. You're probably also really excited to learn more. But at the same time, you have a few self-limiting beliefs going on in that pretty little head of yours. Things that in the past have held you back from the success you deserve.

Things like:

- Calling someone at a bank makes me nervous
- What if the bank says, "no"?
- I'm not good at (or I've never done) public speaking
- What happens if they ask questions, I don't know the answers to
- What if I mess up?

Would you agree that I could go on and on? Even if you don't I can. Because I've been there, done that and will probably go there again and do it again.

Here's the thing. Every little bit of self-doubt you're feeling right now is because of two reasons.

First, what you're learning right now is new. It's outside your comfort zone. And let's be honest, we all love our comfort zone. But when we're asked to stretch outside our comfort zone, we start to freak out a bit.

Second, a lack of confidence. Again, this is something new. So how can you be confident in something you've never done before? Unless you're one of those people who has confidence coming out of their ears – which I am certainly NOT one of them – you may be thinking that this may not be the right fit for you.

Here's the good news.

If you have those feelings, it is 100% natural. And it's okay to feel that way and be nervous, unsure and however else you're feeling.

But if you stick with me through the rest of this book, I promise you that we, yes we, will overcome all your fears and get you on the fast track to becoming a client-generating machine!

Let's take a quick peak at what you're going to learn during our time together.

What You're Going to Learn

This book is going to show you – in detail – everything there is to know about the Client Getting P.L.A.N. including:

- The complete 7-step system
- How to get banks (and other organizations) to agree to work with you and do all the marketing and in many cases pay for lunch
- The secret Presentation Template that you should use and model for your own L&Ls
- Picking the best topic for your presentation
- A secret way to practice your presentation to eliminate all fear and give you Superman confidence
- How to conduct a powerful L&L that gets people chasing you instead of you chasing them
- How to turn this system on or off whenever you need more clients. And yes, sometimes you have to turn it off because you'll have too many clients!
- Swipe files, call scripts and more
- How to convert this to a webinar and put it on autopilot
- Plus a lot more

By the end of this book you'll know the recipe for a repeatable process to help you get more clients whenever you want. You'll be able to plug this system into your business and depending on your time availability and desire to get started quickly can start seeing results in as little as 30-45 days.

Common Mistakes to Avoid While Getting Started

There are three big mistakes people make when getting started that I don't want you to do.

They are:

1. **Rushing through the material.** This is not a race. While this book is not a long one everything in it is there for a reason and has value to the system. Don't skip steps just to get it done.
2. **Not taking action.** This is the problem with most trainings, courses and how-to material like this. People simply read it but never take action. If you don't take action how can you expect to get results? You must be willing to do the steps to get the results you want.
3. **Not getting started now.** Again, this book is not long. It's an easy read. Short and straight to the point. I did my best to eliminate all fluff. With that being said, there is no reason you can't get started right now.

My advice to you is to take your time but take action. Trust in the system. It works if you work it. Above all else, make it fun! This client generation system should not be hard. Or something that you dread. It should be fun. After all you're helping people solve problems! That should make you feel good and keep you motivated. Then add in your personality to the mix and this should be a blast for you!

Are you ready to see what the 7-steps are? Great. Turn the page.

The Seven Steps – Quick Overview

There are seven steps you'll need to perform with this system. Each one is covered in detail in the remaining chapters.

1. Step One: Construct Your Lists
2. Step Two: Contact Your List
3. Step Three: Create Your Presentation
4. Step Four: Customize, Practice and Perfect Your Presentation
5. Step Five: Confirm and Commit
6. Step Six: Convey Your Message and Close Deals
7. Step Seven: Convert to a Webinar

Without further ado, let's get this party started…

Step One – Construct Your Lists

This step is all about building lists. And no, it's not that kind of list building. You know, the online kind. Instead we're going to be focusing on the all-important lists that will help you get started quickly and keep you organized. Don't let this step fool you. While it's not difficult to complete, it is critical to your success.

What you're going to learn in this step is:

- Why you need to create these lists (because just making them aimlessly doesn't make a lot of sense.)
- What lists you do need to create.
- The best way to create them.
- Explore common mistakes and things you need to avoid.
- Discover what not to do because this can be just as detrimental as doing the wrong thing.
- How to end with an action step every single time. Everything about this course is focused on taking action, because every action will bring you one step closer to your goals.

Why These Lists Are So Important

The lists you'll be creating are important for several different reasons. Firstly, it's going to give you a very solid starting point. You're going to be able to start from point A and then, when done with this course, you're going to be at point B. These lists will give you a solid foundation of where to start so you can build on that the entire way.

This is going to help you keep your thoughts and ideas organized, as you'll most likely always be thinking of new ideas. Having lists will help you keep organized without letting all of those ideas overwhelm you. You'll simply be able to add your thoughts and ideas as you go.

The Three Important Lists

By now you're probably thinking, "So what are these lists anyway?" Fair question.

RIGHT NOW TOPICS

The first list is called the "Right Now Topics". These are the topics that you can talk about "right now." For example, you're a marketing consultant and you focus on video marketing because you know that video marketing can really help a small business generate leads. You can talk to anybody about video marketing at any time because it's second nature to you. You're the expert.

That is an example of a Right Now Topic. You might have several Right Now Topics, and that's great. Perhaps you only have one single topic that you'd consider a Right Now Topic. That's okay too. For example, you're the online video marketing expert and that's who you are and what you're known for. Perfect. It doesn't matter if you have one or one hundred Right Now Topics. The most important thing is to identify them.

FUTURE TOPICS

The next list is for topics that are deemed profitable but, for whatever reason, you're unable to talk about it right now. These are called "Future Topics." For instance, perhaps you're a marketing consultant that knows Facebook Ads are hot right now and that they're gaining momentum because so many people use them to generate leads and customers for their business.

You know that maximizing that opportunity could be profitable for your business. However, you don't know much about it, or you know too little about it to be able to speak knowledgeably about it so you don't feel comfortable moving it to the Right Now Topic list. You could put it on the Future Topics list because it would be important for your business at a later date.

BANK CONTACTS

The final list is one that will be made up of your bank contacts, and potential bank contacts.

IMPORTANT: Please remember for this book we are focusing working with banks and doing lunch-and-learn presentations at banks. There are many, many alternatives that we will talk about later. When referring to banks, we're talking about any business entity that you will be using to conduct your lunch-and-learns. Remember that banks and credit unions are one and the same.

Don't get intimated by the thought of having to create this list. You're going to learn everything you'll need to know to make it really easy.

At the end of this step you will have three lists in total:

- Right Now Topics
- Future Topics
- Bank Contacts

Compile Your Lists

To start creating your lists all you need to do is get out a pen and paper or your computer and start entering the required information. It really is as simple as that.

NOTICE: When creating the first two lists, focus on topics. Don't worry or get caught up in thinking of powerful or clever titles. We'll do that later. For now, just focus on topics.

RIGHT NOW TOPICS

Our first list is the Right Now topics. An easy way to generate ideas for this list is to identify what your specialty is. What do people ask you about? It could be anything. The service or product you provide to local businesses should be in this topic list. What do you specialize in?

Your specialty is the thing that separates you from everybody else, and this is where you should place your focus. You can you talk about your specialty in your sleep. You can provide endless answers and talk for hours about your specialty. These are great Right Now Topics.

Another valuable Right Now Topic area are things that will help the businesses the most. While this may sound obvious, sometimes people overlook these topics because they may not be the most profitable for your business. But keep in mind that the key to this exercise is to LIST EVERYTHING. It can all be broken down later and there will be room for everything, including the obvious ideas and the most profitable.

Resist the urge to confine your list to certain topics. There is no wrong topic right now – as long as it meets the Right Now Topic guidelines. List them all.

Lastly, your Right Now Topics need to be something that makes you money. This is the ultimate goal after all, and so it's important that whenever you're speaking to people, it has the potential to make you a profit.

Right Now Topics Checklist

- ❑ What do you specialize in?

- ❑ What do you sell that helps businesses the most?

- ❑ What makes you money?

FUTURE TOPICS

These are topics that you do not yet have a firm enough grasp of to speak to people about. Notice there is an emphasis on the word 'yet'. Some of the topics could be things that you want to learn about. Maybe it is something that interests you, or something you see a future in.

A future topic could be something that is hot right now. Even though its hot right now it still falls into your Future Topics list because you understand the potential of the topic, but you don't quite know enough about it yet to give a lunch-and-learn on it.

Finally, Future Topics also have to be profitable. If there is no money you may want to leave it off your list. However, if it's something that can provide a lot of value to your customers but the profit margin is low then you can put it on the list with a lower priority than some of the others.

TOPIC BENEFITS

One of the things you'll want to do now while you're making your list of topics is to add a comment or two referring to the benefits that topic brings to the business. This doesn't need to be elaborate but should explain why your topic is beneficial. You'll want to do this because it's going to help you explain why that topic is the right one for your bank contact.

When you start talking to banks, one of the main things they're going to want to know is how your proposal is going to benefit their customers. By writing down some benefit statements or even just benefit words - trigger words - it's going to help you communicate the value to your contact. Once these benefits are written down, you'll have your sheet in front of you when you're contacting people so they'll be easy to refer to. Writing them down also decreases the chances that you'll forget these important trigger words.

BANK CONTACTS

The third and final list is the list of bank contacts. The key to this list is that you'll want to make sure you're talking to decisions makers – something that is easier said than done. Ideally, you'll want to talk to Vice Presidents and Branch Managers because these are the people that have the authority to say yes or no to having a lunch-and-learn presentation. You'll learn more about this in Step Two where you'll learn a few tips and strategies to get this done rather easily.

Building your list of bank contacts comes down to two things:

1. Contact friends and family that work at a bank(s)

2. Build a list of target banks in your area

Let's first go over contacting friends and family. Some people get nervous about this because they feel that they are a burden to others when asking for something that's going to help them. The reality of it is that people want to help others. Imagine that a friend came to you asking for help in an area you knew something about. How would you feel? Honored that they asked you, and eager to help? This is exactly how most people feel when their friends and/or family ask them for help.

But why ask friends and family first? The biggest reason is because we all know someone who works at a bank. And doesn't it just make sense to use your personal contacts before calling someone out-of-the-blue? Of course it does.

If you don't know anybody directly that works at a bank, certainly you know a friend or relative that knows somebody that works at a bank. Contacting them and getting a referral means it is no longer a cold call; it's a warm call. That makes all the difference in the world. When you can tell someone that you're calling them because so-and-so told you to, their guard goes down and generally speaking, they'll be happy to talk to you.

If you create this list right the first time *and* actually use it you may never have to worry about seeking bank contacts again. Because once you start doing it and it gets rolling they will refer you to other people. It's like a snowball rolling down a hill that gets bigger and bigger. After a while everyone is a referral and you don't even need the second list building strategy. Which is...

The second list building strategy is to use the good old Internet. Opening Google or Yelp, searching your town for banks and credit unions, finding the contact information and compiling it all into a spreadsheet. Yes this is old school. And yes it still works awesomely!

Sometimes you'll be able to find everything you need with a simple search. Including contact names, phone numbers, addresses and maybe even email addresses.

This list doesn't have to be extensive. Your goal should be to compile a list of fifty different banks and depending on the size of your city, you may have one bank that has over fifty different locations. You could make a list of fifty different branches and communicate with them.

At the end of the day, you only need one contact to agree to do a lunch-and-learn with you. Once you conduct it for them and they see the power of it, they'll be excited to refer you to other contacts that they know.

To make compiling this list even easier you can always outsource it to someone on Upwork.com and Fiverr.com. These are freelancer sites with hundreds of people that would love to do work like this for as little as $20. And most of the time it can be done within 24 hours.

Outsourcing is something we could do a whole course on so it really is beyond the scope of this book. But if this is something you think you might want to try, check out the sites listed above and review their tutorials and Job Description guidelines as these will help you get the best person possible.

A word of warning: don't hire someone that doesn't have any reviews. While you might think, "I'll give this person a shot even though they have no reviews. I'll help them get started," there's a good chance that it will backfire, and you will not get the results you're looking for. You want to hire someone that has done the work before.

One final note on outsourcing. Always negotiate. The freelancers you find on Upwork.com expect to be negotiated with. Sometimes you'll find an excellent freelancer that says my terms are my terms and that is because they're busy enough and they're good enough to charge a price and be firm about it. That's okay, but always try and negotiate so you can get that price down a little bit and save yourself money.

Remember to also always pay through escrow, and *only release funds after the project is completed.* Some providers will want you to pay in milestone payments. For a project like this it doesn't make sense to do that. Some providers will ask for you to pay 50% up front and 50% when the project is done. Never do that. Only pay when the project is completed to your satisfaction.

Common Mistakes to Avoid

The first mistake people make is thinking a topic or a person is not valuable or is insignificant. In other words, they think one of their topics - one of the specialty topics - would not be valuable to the attendee. Don't do that when making your list. Just write it down. You know you can delete it later if you need to. Trying to edit your list as you go just doesn't make any sense because you want to have free rein to write down as much information as possible.

This same principle is true for your bank contacts as well. While you're building your list you may have a person that you're thinking, "This person's not going to amount to anything so why bother putting him on the list?" Or, "This family member doesn't know anybody so I'm not going to contact them." Don't do that! You have no idea what they can and can't do, or who they know or don't know. Do not exclude anyone. You may find a goldmine in the most unlikely person.

Another mistake I see people make is pre-screening their list. This is similar to what I described above but the difference is people who think a bank is too small or too big, so they don't want to contact them.

The final mistake – and one that's made throughout the entire course - is trying to get everything perfect. "Everything needs to be just right before I can move on." Does that sound familiar? It's okay. As Dan Kennedy says, "good enough is good enough." It's much better to get something completed and *then* try to make it better instead of never completing it in the first place because you want it perfect.

Time for Action

Now it's time to get your hands dirty and take some action on the things you just learned. And while this step is simple in theory, do not skip it. It's vital to your success going forward.

Your action item for this step is to simply create your three lists:

- Right Now Topics (with benefit statements or trigger words)
- Future Topics (with benefit statements or trigger words)
- Bank Contacts (ask friends and family and/or compile your list)

So, grab a pen and paper and get started. Or use your favorite computer program. Either way is fine. There is not right or wrong way to do this. The only way to fail is to NOT do it. This exercise will take 30-60-minutes. So why not do it now?

Up Next

Step two is about contacting your bank contact list. Some people get worked up about Step Two because they actually have to talk to people. Remember, if use your friends and family first and every call will be a warm call, an easy call to make.

You'll also have a call script/outline you can use. You can customize it to fit your style and personality and it'll work great!

Take a second now and imagine that after step two you will have at least one lunch-and-learn scheduled. Feel the excitement of presenting to people that not only need your service but are excited to learn from you, the expert. After the lunch-and-learn presentation people will come to you asking for your help. They'll want to hire you!

Step Two - Contact Your List

Now you've got your lists, you're excited, and you're ready to move on to the next step. What exactly does that involve? Taking action on what you've already done! In step two, you're going to start working with those lists you created in step one, and take a step further towards your ultimate goal – getting in the door to make your presentation, and turning those presentations into profits!

Step two involves several different things. First, you'll learn how to develop your USM - *"Unique Sales Message"*. The USM is critically important, but here you'll learn, step-by-step, how to create your own.

You'll also learn how to develop several different call scripts. While they're called scripts, don't get too hung up on that word. Often people are worried that using a script will make you sound fake or phony. This doesn't have to be the case but if it makes you feel better, think of it as an outline.

You'll also learn how to handle "the gatekeeper." Ultimately, you're going to talk to somebody that has a screener, and sometimes you may just be trying to talk to somebody that has a "gatekeeper," or someone screening his or her calls. You'll need to know how to get past that person on the phone to reach the person you ultimately want to talk to, and step two will teach you how to do that.

Once you do reach your desired contact, they'll likely have many questions for you. You may not always know how to answer those questions, especially when you first start out talking to people, but you don't want to appear unknowledgeable, or do anything that will halt the sales process. In step two you'll learn how to handle questions and put it back on them, while still giving some insight to what they're asking. This will keep the conversation going and will keep you on the road to securing that lunch-and-learn.

Step two will also touch on creating a call schedule. This is important because while it's fairly easy to say or think, "Oh, I'll call that person tomorrow or on Friday," there's a much better chance that it will actually get done if you schedule all of your calls, and have it written down somewhere to remind you. It will also make you feel slightly guilty if you don't make a call on a specific day. And that's not necessarily a bad thing.

The System, and Why It's Important

Everything within step two is all part of a system, and that system is extremely important. Firstly, it's important to have a system that you can follow whenever you need it. Once you create this system, you'll be able to use it over and over again as much or as little as you need to.

When done right, you'll be amazed at how after implementing it the first time you may never have to use it again because of all the referrals and momentum you've created. Believe me, this has happened before. But if you do have to go back to it, you'll have the confidence in knowing that it works. Plus, you'll have experience with the implementation and can do it even faster the next time. And probably with greater results.

The system is also important to help you build confidence because you'll know that you have a foundation that is proven to work. You'll be able to practice different techniques and strategies and of course, practice will also build confidence.

This system is also important to help give you a sense of commitment and make you responsible for the follow-through, which in turn means that you'll be more likely to do it and to succeed in doing so. This is really important because that's going to help you reach your goals, which is something you'll want to do as quickly as possible.

What Outcomes Can You Expect?

You're going to be able to create a calling plan and system to follow. Think of it as a **"structure"** instead of "a system" because you'll actually be creating a calling plan and a structure to follow. At the end of this training session, you'll be able to actually make those calls!

Once you have your calling list, your scripts, and your call schedule, you need to then move onto "Next step actions," which may or may not be appointments.

You might hear, *"Let's just schedule a lunch-and-learn right now. We'll test this first one out and see how it goes."* If that's the case, you're ahead of the game and have booked an actual appointment.

However, you may also hear, *"Okay, I need to see you face to face because I like what I hear. But I still need to meet with you first. That's how I operate and it's just a step that I need to go through."*

Both of these scenarios are next step actions and the bottom line is you want a certain number of those. How many that is will ultimately be up to you, but you need to have a firm number of how many "next step actions" you want to have because that's ultimately part of your goal.

In review, you're first going to learn about your unique sales message and how to create it. This will be simple verbiage to help you clearly explain your message to others.

Then you'll learn about the different calling scripts - one for gatekeepers, and one for your primary contact.

Then you'll learn how to answer common questions and how to actually schedule calling time before moving onto the "Next step actions," or the launch and learn.

Your Unique Sales Message

A Unique Sales Message – or USM – is simply a single sentence that explains what you do, who you do it for and what benefits they will get.

The most important thing about creating your USM is that it focuses on them - the bank contact. At this point, the bank contact is your customer. And so, you want to create a message for them.

How do you do that?

You tell them about the benefits that you can provide them. Old-school, traditional marketing is all about you or your business. With this type of marketing you'll hear a lot of, "We've been in business for 20 years; we're the leader in this and the leader that; and we have the most experienced staff." Truthfully? None of that means squat to the customer and so you want to avoid using these types of sales techniques. Instead, you want to create your message for them, because all the bank contact wants really, are two things.

The first is that they want to provide value to their customers. There are only so many things that they can do in order to do that, so they're looking for new and unique ways to bring that value; that's exactly what the system does through lunch-and-learn presentations. The biggest benefit for them is that you're really the one doing it all. It's going to be easy on them and, because banks make so much money, the small cost to them is going to be just that – small.

Again, remember when you're speaking to them to focus on them not you. That's one of the most important things. Then make a quick template, remembering that you can use it and tweak. This template is just something to help guide you through this process.

At the end of the day, all you're doing is helping banks provide needed solutions to their customers through free lunch-and-learn training.

Whatever that training is, whatever *your* area of specialty is, it doesn't really matter. All that matters is that *you* have something to offer their customers that provides value. The first step is to create that first USM. You can always update it, tweak it and change it as you move forward.

USM Template

Here's a fantastic template you can use to create a clear, concise and powerful Unique Sales Message. The beauty of this template is that you can use it over and over again, tweak it, adjust it and just play with it until you get the right one.

> I help *WHO YOU HELP* Do/Understand *WHAT* by *WHAT YOU DO* so that *BENEFITS THEY CAN ACHIEVE*.

USM Example

I help banks (credit unions) provide needed solutions to their customers by doing free lunch-and-learn trainings so that they can continue to offer them great value and grow customer loyalty.

Create Your Own USM

I help _____ Do/Understand _____ by _____ so that _____.

Getting Past the Gatekeeper

Getting through to the right people often calls for an ability to get past the gatekeeper. This is the receptionist, secretary, or personal assistant to the person that you ultimately want to speak to. One of the jobs these people have is to screen calls for their boss, which is often why they're called the "gatekeeper." You'll need to get past this person so that you're not always told your contact is busy, and so that you don't leave countless messages with no return call.

One of the first things you need to do is to ask for your bank contact by name. It sounds much more professional to ask for "Jeff Champion," then it does the "bank's general manager." Asking for the person by name also makes you sound more confident, and even like you may know the person you're asking for. This increases your chances of being put right through to Mr. Champion instead of leaving a message that might eventually get thrown away.

As obvious as it sounds, remember to be nice and approachable when on the phone with anyone. The gatekeeper might be used to getting these types of calls and might be getting a little tired of them. If you're nice and can engage them in casual, friendly conversation, you might just make yourself stand out from the crowd. Many of the people the gatekeeper will speak to will be on their 200th phone call of the day – and maybe you are, too. But the difference between you and them will be that you don't show it – in your voice, in your tone, or in your words. At this point in the sales calls many people start to become harsh and abrasive because they're getting a bit fed up themselves. Don't let that be you. Always be nice, always be approachable, and you may just be surprised at how far that gets you.

Remember though, that engaging them doesn't mean to keep them on the phone any longer than they have to be. It means you need to keep it simple but friendly. And if you know their name, try to use it. Something such as, *"Hi, Beth I'm hoping you can help me out. Is Jeff Champion available?"* It's super simple, super straightforward and a lot of times it'll get you passed right through.

Be prepared however, they may ask you some questions, starting with your name. They are also likely to ask you, *"May I ask, what this is regarding?"* This is all part of their screening process, so this is an important question to answer – but it's crucial *how* you answer it. You want to answer their question, but you also want to make sure you don't answer anything that they haven't asked. So while you may briefly tell them your unique sales message, you also don't want to go into too much detail, or give them more than they asked for.

Once you've told them a little bit about your sales message, another good strategy is for you to ask, "*Would you be someone who would help with this decision or should I speak with Jeff Champion?*"

This is a critical question that you really don't want to amend and here's why. It takes the focus off of you and puts it on them. The chances are that they don't have the authority to make the decision to bring you in for a presentation, and they won't want to do or say anything that would make it appear that they have that authority. By asking, "*Would you be someone who would help with this decision?*" you'll most likely hear in response something similar to "*Oh no, no, no, no. I do not have anything to do with that. Let me pass you on through to Jeff*". That's typically how this scenario plays out, so while you can change it up to your own liking. It's proven to be extremely effective.

Call Script / Outline

Now that you've made it past the gatekeeper and with your new, powerful USM in hand it's time to talk to your contact. But what do you say?

The first thing you don't want to do is don't start with, "*I'm calling banks in your area.*" People want to feel like they're the only person you are calling. When you say **"I am calling banks in your area"** they immediately know that they were put on a list and is one of many calls you'll be making that day. They won't stand out to you and in return, you won't stand out to them. But what you can do is start with, "*Hi Jeff, my name is (such-and-such – make sure you use your first and last name.*" This is simple and straightforward, and it will likely continue the flow of conversation.

After you introduce yourself, explain why it is that you are calling. Remember to tell them about a need that *they* have, whether it's getting new customers or expanding on customer loyalty. Then make sure to explain how *you* can help provide the solution to that need – through your lunch-and-learn presentations. You then continue by saying, "*I'd *like to ask you a few questions to see if this is something, you'd like more information on"* or, *"I'd like to ask you a few questions to see if this is a good fit."*

So, for example, your call script might look something like:

"Hi Jeff, I'm Charles Johnson and I might have something for your customer relations department that could add a lot of value to your customers. I can also do this at no charge to you. I'd like to ask you a few questions to see if this is something, you'd like more information on. Can I ask those questions now? It will only take two minutes."

When you use this as a guideline or script, there will be enough intrigue there for your contact to want to learn more. This is because what you're actually saying is, *"Give your customers something that they want and need and do it at no cost to you."* The chances are good that they're going to say, *"Okay, you have my interest. Tell me how you're going to do it."* That's when you're going to explain what the lunch-and-learn process is all about.

Leaving Effective Voicemail Messages

Even with the best script or guideline, you won't get passed the gatekeeper every time. Ultimately, you're going to end up leaving a lot of voicemails – and maybe speaking to more voicemails than live contacts - so it's important to have a structure to the voice mail message you'll leave.

Having a structure will make you more confident, and that will help you get return calls. If nothing else, they'll recognize your voice when you call them for a follow-up. Leaving a voice mail message can be as easy as:

"Hi Jeff, I'm Charles Johnson with Johnson Marketing. When I was speaking with Beth, she said you were the person I should speak with regarding new ways of adding value for your customers. We've been able to help other banks in similar situations add massive value to their customers while increasing loyalty, and we're able to do it at no charge to you, or your customers. I'd like to ask you a few questions to see if what we have might be a good fit. I'll try you again on Friday. In the meantime, you can always call me at [your phone number] or email me at [your email address]. Thank you. Have a great day!"

This dialogue is friendly but simple, and it tells them why you're calling, but doesn't go into great detail.

This last part is important because you want them to still need to speak to you so that they'll return your call or speak to you the next time you call them.

Talking Points

You've gotten to the point where you have your contact on the phone, you've asked if you can go through a few questions with them, and they've said "yes." Now what?

The first question should be, "Have you ever used an expert to provide free lunch-and-learn trainings to help your customers solve a problem or educate them on a specific topic?" There are only two answers they'll have for you – either "yes," or "no."

No matter what they answer, you can come back with, "We've discovered that this is a great way to provide massive value to your customers while in turn building a strong sense of loyalty among your customers." And then you simply go into "Let me quickly explain what I do and how it can benefit you", and then you describe what you do - free lunch-and-learns - how you do it at their location, and a few other things to discuss.

You want to make sure that you have an outline to follow here, and within that outline the benefits the presentations will bring the bank, and how it will provide value to the customers in a unique way. Always remind your contact how much value there is within that presentation, and that it would be free to both them and their customers.

Then simply follow-up with, **"Do you think this is something that you like to discuss further?"**

If they do, great! Then it's just a matter of setting up an appointment to speak with them face-to-face.

If they say "no," or they have questions, continue to explain how the lunch-and-learn works.

So, how do they work?

What They Provide for the L&L

One of the first things they'll want to know is what they need to provide for these lunch-and-learns. Here are some talking points:

- It's going to be at their facility, so they don't have to rent a room or have added expenses of doing that.
- They should have a projector or HDTV you can connect your computer to so you shouldn't have to worry about lugging one around.
- You should always ask them to provide lunch with drinks or at a minimum, offer to split the cost of that with you. Try to get them to cover the cost entirely as, even with a maximum of 25 people in attendance, this will be a very low cost to the bank.
- They should be the ones doing the promotion for it. These are their customers attending, so in a sense they're kind of your joint venture partner for this lunch-and-learn so they should do all the promotion whether it's by email or direct mail, they should be responsible for any costs associated with that.

What You Provide for the L&L

Of course, you can't just show up and hope that's enough. After all, there will be people that have gathered there to hear *you* speak. So, what do you need to provide to them, and to the bank?

- Training on your specific topic is essential of course, because this is what the entire presentation will be about.
- You should also bring anything that you'll need specifically for the presentation. These can be things like handouts, name tags or name tents on tables.
- Having a printed book or report is really powerful at this point because it does two things. Firstly, it's awesome to have a handout on the subject or topic so that you can talk about it during your lunch-and-learn. If at the end of the presentation, you can hand them a professionally bound report or booklet, it will keep you and your training in their minds, as well as look especially impressive to the bank so they'll want to have you back again. It will take you one step further to becoming viewed as the expert on this particular topic.

Answering Questions

It's difficult to guess all of the different scenarios and questions that you're going to come across because everybody's different, and its amazing how different responses can be given at any one time.

However, you're going to be asked some questions that you're not sure how to answer. When that happens you can respond with,

"I'm not sure. How do you see that playing out?" or, "I'm not sure. What do you prefer?" Or you can use, "Well typically, that is handled by either you or the customer."

However, you answer the question, no matter what question is asked, always end it with, "Does that work for you?" or "What do you prefer?"

For example, if they're asking, "Who pays for lunch?" you would answer, "Well typically, that is handled by the bank. Does that work for you?" This is very low-pressure and non-invasive. What you're saying is that this is the way it's done, this is the way everyone else does it, and there's really no reason why it shouldn't work for them – but you're saying it without being pushy, and still making sure it works for the bank.

Make sure that, as you're being asked questions, you write them down; and also write down the answers you gave. The chances are good that you'll be asked this question again and adding to the list of them will let you study them, research them, and be more prepared the next time you're asked the same thing. You'll also always be able to think of more ways to bring their questions right back to one of the benefits they'll receive by having you in for a presentation.

Schedule Calling Time

You need to schedule a time to call your contacts, and you need to do it now. You need to put it in your calendar and commit to it just like anything else you schedule in your life, whether it be an actual appointment with a bank or a dentist appointment.

Schedule your calling time and then commit to it. Because your goal is to have each contact you're going to call commit to the next action. It only makes sense that you commit yourself as well.

There are one of three outcomes that you'll want to achieve:

> ➢ Schedule a face-to-face meeting,

> ➢ Schedule an actual lunch-and-learn,

> ➢ Determine the contacts that are not interested. Remove these people from your contact list and move on, happy in the

knowledge that you don't have to waste any more time on them.

Of course, you want them to commit to whatever that next action is. You don't want them saying, "Well I need to think about it", so do your best to schedule a face-to-face meeting.

Key Tip: Make sure they understand that THEY will be fully responsible for the promotion of the presentation. After all, the attendees of the presentation will be their customers and only they have access to their customer database. They are not going to give you that access, nor should they, so they should be expected to do the promotion. You can make this easier on them by already having promotional swipes files that you've customized for the event. Then you can tell them, "I already have these things together. They're already printed up, so you would just have to put them in the mail," or, "I already have this email file that can be sent as promotion." This will show your contact that you've already done the hard part. All they have to do is send them out.

Common Mistakes to Avoid

The first few times people do this; they sometimes make common mistakes. While mistakes are really just lessons, you can avoid them altogether by knowing what they are and making sure you avoid them whenever possible.

Firstly, know that most mistakes are made when people do not follow the system. Remember that the wheel does not need to be reinvented here. This is a proven process just follow it and trust that it will work *because it will.*

Another big mistake is being reluctant to make the call, especially with people that may feel uncomfortable talking to strangers on the phone. They become reluctant, and they make excuses to keep putting off those phone calls. Don't let that be you! Fight through it, start making calls and soon you'll realize that it isn't that bad, and that you've got this.

Worried about not being able to answer every possible question every single time? Remember that's okay. You can always get back to your contact with the correct answer.

And then another common mistake is trying to get it perfect before you even get started. Ninety-nine percent of the stuff you imagine in your head never comes true so there's really no point in worrying about it too much. Fight through, power on, and get the work done.

What Not to Do

There are a lot of things you need to do. But what should you avoid doing?

- Don't make excuses as to why you can't start right now. There is no good reason for not starting your contact list and getting on the phone right now, so just get it done.
- Don't overthink it. Again, trust in the system, trust in the process, and just take action.
- Do not use a call service (not yet anyway.) If you use a call service at this point, you don't know what's going to work best in your area. Once you start using the call scripts and speaking to a few people, you'll have a better idea as to what will work and what will not. Do it for a month or two, and you'll be able to replay the conversation in your head before it's even happened. If at that point you want to use a call service, that's up to you, but don't do it before then. Even when you can foresee how the conversation will go, it's always better to make the calls yourself. Not only will it make the call more personal, it will also help you if there ever comes a time when you'd like somebody else to do it. You'll be able to coach them and educate them and explain what they can expect and how to overcome certain things.

Time for Action

Now it's time to take action. The first thing you'll need to do is create your lists. All of them!

The second thing you need to do is write your unique sales message. Go ahead and do that. Create as many as you need to make you feel comfortable. Don't be afraid to change it up; don't limit yourself. Just open your mind and be as creative as you can.

Third, customize and practice the calling scripts for both the gatekeeper and your actual contact.

Lastly, plan your calling schedule and stick to it. It's a beautiful thing.

Up Next

Next up is step three. In this step you'll learn how to create your presentation. It's okay to schedule the presentation before you've even created it so that you'll at least know that people are interested and want to see it. Go ahead and make your calls now.

Then move onto step three and learn some presentation basics, how to build confidence, and how to provide a powerful presentation. It's not going to be a long 60-minute boring presentation. Instead, it's going to be 20 to 40-minutes, tops. This will allow for a question-and-answer period, and different networking opportunities.

Step Three - Create Your Presentation

Now is the time to create your killer presentation, and you'll learn how to do that in Step Three. This guideline for your lunch-and-learn presentations are proven to work well in these types of situations, and by following this guideline your presentation won't only be effective, it will be interesting to your audience, and they will not become bored by it.

What You'll Learn

Firstly, you'll learn how to write an irresistible title. The title of your presentation is very similar to the title of a book. The title of a book captures your interest and makes you want to read that book. It's the same thing with the title of your presentation. It has that same effect so it's important to get it right. You'll also learn the basics of lunch-and-learn presentations, because they're different than other types of presentations. Getting the basics down will allow you to be more engaging and effective.

You'll also learn how to create an outline for your presentation. You want to make sure that you're only including things that are absolutely necessary, and that it doesn't end up being a presentation about you and your company for 60-minutes. That is boring, and no one cares, nor wants to sit through that! What people care about is how they can get their problems solved, so your presentation should be full of those solutions.

You'll also learn about "presentation enhancers," and how to add them to your presentation. These enhances will increase audience engagement and keep you from speaking in a monotone, boring voice, while throwing a bunch of facts at them. This is not engaging or fun or enlightening to the attendees. These enhancers will help you avoid those potential pitfalls.

You're inevitably going to come across non-believers, and this chapter you'll learn how to handle them. No matter what, in every lunch-and-learn presentation there is usually one person who is a non-believer and tries to throw road blocks in front of you. This chapter will cover those so you're prepared and know how to deal with them when they happen.

Why This is Important

Having an organized and properly structured lunch-and-learn presentation is important, because without it, you risk having a negative response to your presentation. If your presentation flops, that is a poor reflection on you and the chances are slim that anyone in the room would want to do business with you.

You are the one doing a lunch-and-learn presentation, and you are supposed to be the expert on the topic. Because of this, you need to have a presentation that's properly structured to prove that you in fact are the trusted advisor.

Remember that creating a powerful presentation only has to be done once, because if you do it right the first time you can use it over and over again. There's no need to create a new presentation every single time. Get it right the first time and use it for all your lunch-and-learns.

How to Write an Irresistible Title

Let's start writing irresistible titles by giving you a template, or several templates, in which you can just fill-in-the-blanks. Below are some examples.

- 'How to <u>Accomplish Specific Result</u> in <u>XX Days or Less</u> Without <u>Pain the Want to Avoid</u>." For example, "How to

Attract All the Clients You Can Handle in 30-Days or Less Without Cold Calling!"

- 'X steps to accomplishing something.' This can be 7 steps to Market Your Business, 10 Ways Mobile Marketing Can be Easier for You, or whatever your specialized field or area is. The important part of this title is that you're providing them with a concrete number of ways to do something, and that all of them will be beneficial to whatever they're trying to do.
- 'Secrets Revealed.' These are the "secrets" everyone should know about whatever service you're offering. If you're giving a presentation on creating a website, the title of your presentation could be, "Website Secrets Revealed: The 10 Things Web Hosts Don't Want You to Know." This dynamic title tells your audience right away that just by attending your presentation, they'll learn things that they otherwise never would have known.
- "The Top 'Blank'." This one is quite generic, but the beauty of that is that you can make it whatever you want it to be. It can be the top ways to make the most money possible when selling your home, the best ideas for starting a small business, or the "best" or "top" ways of doing anything else you think is relatable to your presentation.

As you can see, these are four easy-to-use but powerful templates that you can use. All you have to do is fill-in-the-blanks on your topic and the benefits it gives to the attendees and the problems it solves. Let's go over a few more examples to get your wheels spinning even more.

The first example is the famous book, "How to Win Friends and Influence People." This is kind of a generic example, but you can see the power in a simple 'how to' title.

The next example is what I used for the Client Getting PLAN, "Seven Steps to Getting All the Clients you can Handle without Cold Calling or Spending a Dime on Marketing". You can see that there are a certain number of steps (7) to getting the ultimate goal that they want (getting all the clients they can handle.) This title goes one step further by explaining that it can be done without the pains and problems that quickly come to mind with client acquisition (without cold calling or spending a dime on marketing). You can see that is a very powerful title because there is immediate intrigue. It makes you wonder what those 7 steps are. It goes another level deeper by covering a huge pain point of cold-calling. Which is common practice in a lot of client acquisition models. But something most – if not all – people dread doing.

The next title is the "Mobile Marketing Secrets Every (city you are in) Small Business Should Know". Although this is somewhat generic, you can narrow that down as much as you would like. Call it "The Ten Mobile Marketing Secrets Every Small Business Should Know". Each title will be different depending on what your topic is, the benefits it provides and the problem it solves, but you can plug and play with a lot of these different things.

Another one is, the "Top Ten Marketing Strategies for Dallas Businesses". Again, it's the top 10 so people that are struggling with growing their business are going to want to know what the top 10 marketing strategies are. You can also say the "Top Ten Marketing Strategies for 2019". This would be even more powerful because it's specific for an upcoming time frame.

All of these types of titles will work for your lunch-and-learn presentation and garner the attention of potential attendees. Do not make it more difficult than what it needs to be. Simply use these templates, go through the process, create multiple titles and then pick the best one. It does not have to be overly complicated.

Lunch-and-Learn Basics

There are some basics that you want to follow when making a lunch-and-learn presentation. The first thing is that it needs to be short but powerful. Remember that 'lunch' is right in the title – it needs to be over lunch. It's not going to be a three-hour workshop or seminar, it's going to be strictly over lunch, and that's why the presentation needs to be short and sweet.

Depending on your solution and what you are presenting, it could be as little as 20-minutes, but make sure that it is no longer than 40-minutes. You really need to cut out the fat and give them only the meat and potatoes, so-to-speak. They do not want to sit there for 60-minutes listening to you talk about your business, your company and how great you are.

They want to come and have one of their problems solved. If you can cut it down to 20-minutes and leave the remaining time for Q&A, that is very powerful. Even if you go to 40-minutes, that is okay too as long as you leave enough time for Q&A.

Ultimately, there will be a lot of questions and you'll need time to answer them. Don't think of it as a 60-minute session, even though that is typically the amount of time people have for lunch. Chances are it will go longer. And that's what you want. Because that means the people who are interested will stick around and want talk with you one-on-one.

On the flip side, some of the people that will be in attendance may not have more than an hour and might not even be the decision-maker. They may simply be going back to the decision-maker with the knowledge that they've learned during your presentation. Which is fine too.

If the decision maker is in attendance, they might be able to be there for much longer, but you do not want to take up their valuable time with a long drawn out presentation. The only way your presentation should exceed the 60-minute mark is because of Q&A and networking.

One Problem, One Solution

Another basic of L&L's you want to focus on is one problem that the audience is facing, and one solution for that problem. For example, as a marketing consultant you can talk about video marketing. You can explain to them the different video marketing strategies, the various types of videos that work with each strategy and show them actual videos, so they can see for themselves how it all comes together.

I'm sure you can agree that this is extremely powerful. But you can take it a step further and go deeper into one single video marketing strategy for an even bigger impact. For example, I can argue that EVERY business needs an explainer video.

Imagine, a L&L that focuses on what explainer videos are, why they work so well, how every business needs one and then show them real world examples. Do you see how powerful this is?

In a nutshell, this is an example of one problem, one solution. You aren't talking about video marketing and also including email and postcard marketing, landing pages and how to make your website more responsive. That's about five different problems! Instead, resist the temptation to talk about everything all-at-once, and simply focus on one problem, one solution.

The cool thing about that is it keeps you focused, and it keeps your attendees interested. They know exactly what to expect. If you are able to offer multiple solutions, you can create a lunch-and-learn solution of each one, so you have a lot more content. And you'll be able to provide these presentations over and over again all on different topics. This is very powerful because ultimately your bank contacts are going to want to have you mix it up a little bit instead of presenting the same thing every month.

Another basic of L&L's is to avoid putting your logo on every slide. Doing so is not only old school and outdated, it's also redundant and comes off as 'in your face,' advertising and promotion. When bringing slides in as part of your presentation, put your logo on one of the first slides and one at the end. This will give the audience enough information to know how to contact you, and that's really all you need. Anything else will be overkill. Especially since you'll be providing a handout.

Important Things to Include in Your Presentation

There are many important things to include in your presentation, but you want to start off talking about why you're the one to help with their problem. Some people like to cover a few things first, such as statistics, before moving onto the "why you" section. That's fine if this is what you want to do, but the most important thing to remember is that you limit this section to the direct benefits of what you are talking about.

For example, if you are talking about mobile marketing, you want to talk about the benefits you bring to them as a mobile marketing expert and why they should trust you to be the one to tell them what to do. You do not need to go into all the details of miscellaneous certifications and degrees and whatever else that you have that may have nothing to do with mobile marketing. You can say you have been in business for 'x' number of years, but don't go overboard when it comes to talking about your experience. Ultimately, no one cares.

Again, you want to talk about why you are here, and what you hope they get out of your presentation. Make sure you have a section on the presentation outline titled "What you are going to learn" or something similar.

Avoid calling this outline an "agenda," because once someone reads 'agenda,' they immediately start thinking it's very professional and institutional or corporate.

You want to avoid this, as it's a lunch-and-learn presentation and should be in a relaxed atmosphere and hopefully kind of fun. Also, attendees may think it's your agenda towards them, and it's not a mutual thing. Instead you want to phrase it as 'What We Are Going to Learn', or 'Today's Goals' or "What We'll Cover Today'. Any of these, or a variation of them, typically helps break down the walls that they put up before the presentation even gets started.

The next thing to cover is why the topic is important and the benefits it will bring to them. You want to make sure that they understand exactly why, how and which ways the information you are going to present to them will be beneficial to them.

Once you've introduced yourself and told them what benefits they'll get from your presentation, it's time to get down to the actual content of your presentation. This should be about 75% - 80% of your presentation.

In the example, "The Client Getting Plan," it's 7-steps, and these 7-steps can be covered in about 20-minutes at a very high-level overview. For the most part, the presentation in a lunch-and-learn environment has a length of 20 to 40-minutes. Of which, 80% of that time, or maybe a little more, should be dedicated to the main content.

Lunch-and-learn presentations are very effective when presented in a step by step format because it's logical, it makes sense and you can apply it to almost any topic. If you are doing a top 10 list of some sort, for example, the "Top Ten Marketing Strategies of 20XX", you would simply go through 1 to 10. Here it would not necessarily be steps, but rather major points and concepts. But it would still be structured in a way that they can follow along logically, and it makes sense to them.

Within the main content, you'll also want to include 'common mistakes'. There are things that customers or prospects may try to do if they are following your presentation. If you're giving a presentation on explainer videos, they might try to go out and do it themselves. (This rarely happens but you still want to cover the common mistakes to better position you as the expert and someone who is there to help them be successful.) When they do, they will make mistakes. It's a guarantee because they are not the expert. You want to tell them about these mistakes, and how to avoid them. Again, mostly likely they will not try to do it on their own. But if they do, they'll know that you want to help them out. And that builds credibility and trust.

You also want to present these mistakes in such a way that it gets them thinking, 'Wow! I can see myself making these mistakes and I do not want to do that. I need to hire the expert to do it."

Of course, you always have to follow up with an action step. If you only give them the information and do not give them something to do with that information, they are going to leave that presentation thinking the content was good, but something was missing. Worse, they will not know what to do next or where to go. That action step should be something they need to do on their own, but also make sure to tell them that if they have any questions, they can contact you and you will help walk them through it.

Of course, your presentation doesn't have to follow the format of, "Why me," "Benefits," and "Main Content." You can mix them up and change them as you see fit and follow along according to what fits your presentation style and personality. This is simply an outline to tell you what's important to include, and to give you a good starting point as your foundation.

Want a pre-made PowerPoint template built specifically for the Client Getting Plan presentation style? You can download one here:

ClientGettingPlan.com/toolkit

Presentation Enhancers

Presentation enhancers are things that will help you engage your audience and add a little more 'oomph' to your presentation.

Images are one of the main presentation enhancers that are used, but it's very important to make sure that any images you use are relatable.

For example, if you're talking about a mobile marketing site and you have a dog, showing a picture of the dog is not relatable and does not make sense. When the message is relatable however, it helps remain in the audience's mind and reinforces the idea. It's crucial to make sure every single image you use is relatable and that you use them only when trying to really emphasize a single point.

Consider using screenshots for some of your images. For example, if you are talking about how to use a program or plug in, you can take screenshots of it and use them as part of your presentation. That will help reinforce the message you are trying to get across.

Stories are also presentation enhancers. When you can tell a story to help explain your point it's extremely powerful and will make more of an impact than simply stating why your audience should do it. If you equate the "why" with a story, the attendees will relate to you, be engaged, and also be intrigued.

Don't get so lost in the structure that you forget to show off your personality. Make sure you use it to your full advantage. If you're an outgoing and fun-loving person, you don't want to restrain that personality. Instead, embrace it and allow everyone else to see it.

Lastly, one type of presentation enhancer that is very powerful is a single page, fill-in-the-blanks worksheet. These increase the engagement and retention of the attendees.

All you need to do is create a fill-in-the-blank worksheet based on your presentation slides. It can be done in Word, it doesn't need to cover every slide or every point, and you can make the fonts a little bigger. Have them follow along so that they need to fill-in-the-blanks.

At the end, they have all the information on that one-page. Keeping it to a single page will make it easy to use and follow along. It can include front and back if you'd like, but you want to make it one page only on thick colored card stock. It can be printed from a home computer or from a professional printer.

Handling Non-Believers

The non-believers in your crowd (at some point there will be at least one) are nothing to get too worried about, but you do need to know how to handle them. Non-believers are not necessarily those that "don't believe you," per se, but rather, they're people that may think their business is so different and unique that the solution you are offering will not work for them. You need to be able to approach these people in a professional and non-confrontational way.

There are really two ways to do it.

The first is to acknowledge, appreciate and acquire more information. For example, someone tells you that their business is so different that what you're saying will not work for them. You respond with "I appreciate that Mr. Customer; may I ask why you feel your business is different?" Or, "I totally understand and appreciate what you are saying, but why do you feel this will not work for your business?" Then let them explain their reasoning.

To that response you might say something simple such as, "In my experience, I have had customers in similar situations and their results have been great! In fact, ..." Then continue explaining what happened in that similar situation. Remember that you need to make sure you talk about a similar situation; you do not want to make stuff up.

However, you can see that this flow is more conversational versus confrontational. You want to put their mind at ease. You need to acknowledge and appreciate them and, in some cases, you need to acquire more information.

Another way to think about this approach is what's known as "feel, felt, found." Basically, it sounds like this, "Mr. Customer, I totally understand how you feel. In fact, I had a customer in a similar situation as yours and he felt the same way. But what he found out was that our solution worked extremely well for him because…" This is a great approach because it shows your prospect that they are not alone, but it also overcomes the object at the same time.

Another way to handle non-believers is to acknowledge and appreciate it, then move on. For example, "You know, Mr. Customer, I understand what you are saying, and I really appreciate it, however, quite frankly our solution is not a good fit for everyone. Maybe that is the case here. I would not know unless we were to sit down and talk a little bit more. Perhaps we can do that after…" Then you simply move on.

For some people, this is not the most comfortable way to go about things, but it's very powerful. This is because when someone resists what you are offering, and you respond with "maybe it's not the right fit", it suddenly takes a solution away from them. They realize that, and 9 times out of 10 they'll reach out for that solution again. It's really a "take-away" close. "Well it may not be the right fit for you and that is okay." They'll respond with, "What do you mean it's not the right fit? I did not say that. I am just saying my business is different."

From there you can talk about it more or ask them to table it until after the Q&A session is over, and then be able to move on from there.

Common Mistakes to Avoid

During the course of creating your presentation, you are bound to make some mistakes. That is, unless you know what they are and how to avoid them from the start.

Firstly, make sure you're creating a presentation that's about them and not you. Remember it's about one problem, one solution that you can help them with. It's not all about you and your company.

Another common mistake is adding too much information and making the lunch-and-learns too long. You do not want to just compile so much information that when they leave, they are thinking, 'Holy cow I think that was a good presentation, but I have no idea because there was so much information. I am so confused'.

Another common mistake to avoid is not leaving enough time for Q&A. This goes hand-in-hand with adding too much information because only having 5 or 10 minutes for Q&A is generally a result of having too much information and making your presentation too long. This does not benefit you because you want some time for Q&A.

Inevitably they are going to have questions and you want to be able to answer them. You want to allow enough time for Q&A so you can elaborate on whatever they may have questions on. Then, if there is time at the end of that Q&A, people will approach you or ask you more specific questions about their business. This is when you can start setting up appointments.

That also leads into the next common mistake, which is not giving the audience any time to come up and talk to you. You want them to approach you at the end of the Q&A. You want them to come up, chat with you and say "Hey I really want to talk to you. I have to leave now, but how can we connect"? You want to give everyone, anywhere from 10, 15, 20, 25 people maximum, the opportunity to come and talk to you. Most people will leave right away but some will stay and want to discuss next steps.

Avoid another common mistake by bringing them a valuable giveaway. You need to give them something, and the fact that they're getting it can be included as part of the promotional material as well. When the bank sends out the email or direct mail letter it can include "Joey is going to give away his free book (audio or DVD) to everyone that attends". Creating a book, DVD or audio program is a lot easier than you think.

SIDE NOTE: Have you ever wanted to write and publish your own print book? They're still the best way to build trust, credibility and authority in your marketplace and its actually easy to do. Check out my site for more details:

CredibilityBook.com

If you can make it a little different from the topic you are covering, it's very impactful because it looks like they are getting two trainings and content pieces for one.

Even if you are repurposing the same content but with a different twist, the perception is still that they are getting more than just a regurgitation of the presentation they just saw. Doing so can also help make your presentation more concise because you say things like, "Listen to my CD on the way back to your office, and you will discover these secrets ..." Say this at the end of your presentation so that it's fresh in their minds and they'll actually listen to it. You can create a CD at Kunaki.com and it only costs less than a cup of gas station coffee to get a professional CD or DVD created.

What Not to Do

The biggest "not-to-do" is only making it about you and your company. Of course, you'll need to include that, but it should not be the focus.

Also, do not go into excruciating detail about your topic. Cover the highlights and help them solve one single problem instead of covering 18 different things. That will just confuse and overwhelm them.

Do not feel as though your presentation is too short. As long as you've solved a problem for them, 20-minutes presentations over lunch is fine.

Aim for 35 or 40-minutes, but if it's over the 40-minutes mark, cut out certain slides or talk about fewer things. You really want to make sure you are between that 20 – 40-minute mark.

Time for Action

That's it! You're ready to create your presentation! Time to create a killer title; that is the first thing you need. You want to create a great title for your presentation and the best way is to create a bunch of them and pick the best few, tweak them as much as you need, then let them sit for a day or two then go back to them and the best one will rise to the top.

Secondly, if you've downloaded the CGP Toolkit (see Tools and Resources at the end of this book) you can use the included PowerPoint/Keynote template to create you first lunch-and-learn presentation. You can do that right now, even without a title.

In fact, some people suggest you create your title after you have your content created because you will know more about certain benefits or issues, and things will stand out more. This can help create a more natural title.

Thirdly, create a single page fill-in-the-blanks worksheet. It should not have your slide, but rather it should highlight certain bullet points that you used. That's all you need to do, you don't need to over think it. It's beneficial to use and to get printed on card stock. It's powerful stuff.

Up Next

Congratulations, you made it through Step 3! The next module is Step 4 – To Customize, Practice and Perfect your Presentation. There you'll learn how to practice your presentation effectively, and how to easily customize it for each and every presentation you give.

In Step 4 you'll also learn about the confidence that follows practicing and that is really what matters most. Public speaking is all about confidence and when you know for a fact that you can do it and do it well, your confidence will build to the point that makes any butterflies disappear.

Let's move on to Step 4 now.

Step Four - Customize, Practice and Prepare

In Step 4 you're going to discover the secrets of how to practice your presentation effectively. There is a method to the madness of practicing and preparing for what lies ahead and at this point in time, you most likely have a lot of questions and anxiety. Many people build up the presentation so much in their head that it only causes more nerves than necessary. Those things will all be covered in this step, so you can feel a little more at ease about this whole thing.

What You'll Learn

This step covers all of this and more:

> There will be certain things that you need to customize, and this chapter will go over each one of those, so they're not missed.

> Practicing Best Practices. There is a way to do it that will really enhance your live presentations based on the way that you practice.

> Preparing for your lunch-and-learns. There are a lot of things that you need to know, and you likely have a lot of questions. Being prepared for them will get you off on the right foot.

> Surprises are rarely good in a lunch-and-learn setting. In this chapter you'll also learn what some of those surprises might be, and how to be prepared for them.

Why this is Important

Practice may not make perfect, but it does build confidence, and confidence is the key success factor when it comes to public speaking. This is because when you are the person doing the speaking, you are considered the expert, the guru. What comes with that is when people are new to public speaking or speaking in front of groups in a lunch-and-learn type setting, they get nervous.

They often feel that maybe the audience knows as much as they do or, in some cases, even more. This is never the case, because the audience wouldn't be there if they felt as though they couldn't learn from you. But the reason that some of these self-doubting thoughts appear is because of a lack of confidence. This is why practicing is so important. It gives you the confidence you need.

Customizing Your Presentation

Depending on what you're doing your presentation on and the audience involved, you may require more customization than others. But these ideas are the most common items that you need to make sure that you customize for each presentation.

These customizations will all be based on your "basic" or "core" presentation. But you'll need to customize that presentation, or tweak it, for different lunch-and-learns. The chances are good that you'll be doing a presentation on the same topic more than once, so it's nice to have a foundation, and customize it for different settings.

For example, if you're a marketing consultant and you're talking about mobile marketing, you would take that same presentation but customize it for each individual lunch-and-learn that you do at each different bank. Remember that different topics need different presentations all together. But there's no reason you can't use the same presentation for the same topic.

When customizing your presentation, the first thing you need to do, depending on how your lunch-and-learn is set up, you need to make sure that you change the target audience or change your approach to the target audience.

This is important because you want to make sure that you customize it for every new crowd. If you're a restaurant expert for instance, you want to make sure you're speaking to a restaurant-industry-only crowd; and that your presentation has been customized for that group.

On the other hand, if you have a mixture of small businesses and your presentation is on how small businesses can benefit from going online, you can make it a bit more general.

The one thing in your presentation that you want to make sure you customize every single time is the bank thank you slide. You want to make sure you thank them for being there and for being your "sponsor" for the presentation. You definitely don't want to say something like, "I want to thank ABC bank," when the slide shows XYZ bank.

You need to make sure that all content within your presentation is relatable content, and this may require some customization. Go back to the example of preparing a presentation for restaurant-industry types.

You may give a presentation to them that could be slightly changed and applied to small businesses of all types. You'll need to take the information that is restaurant-specific and make it more relatable to small businesses as a whole.

Your call to action slide is another area that you might want to consider customizing. If you're testing different calls to actions, change up your slides. This could be a great way to see what works best and what garners the best response, whether it's testing out a product, signing up for a free consultation, or taking a survey

Practicing Your Presentation - Best Practices

The core of step four is really Practicing Best Practices. The success or failure of your presentation largely depends on practicing. You can't over emphasize the importance of it. Luckily, there are many techniques and strategies you can employ.

The first thing is to record yourself on video. Often people get really nervous about that because they don't like to see themselves on video, and that's understandable. But it is super important to do because it helps out so much when you are able to see yourself present the information.

You should practice your presentation at least 10 to 15 times (at minimum,) and then record yourself at least 5 of those. Look at the first one compared to the last one, and you'll see how much better it is. It is truly amazing, and on a side note, you can use this opportunity to tweak it as needed to fit into the 20 to 40-minute range.

You'll likely be shocked at just how different the videos are from each other. One might take 55 minutes, while one might only take 15. In one you might sound confident, while in another you may sound shaky.

Decide which one you like best and extract the audio from it. Listen to it in your car, at night, whenever is a good opportunity for you to really listen to it. It will quickly become like you're listening to your favorite song. You know, when you're singing along to it and not missing a beat. It will become that ingrained, and that will help you pull off a flawless presentation. You'll literally know your presentation inside and out.

This is a really important step, because it's one that makes your presentation second nature to you. You can still tweak it however you need to over time, but the bottom line is it is really powerful to be able to hear yourself. That's really how you're going to learn it.

Once you've practiced on yourself, you then want to practice in front of an audience, if given the opportunity. The audience doesn't have to be big; one person is fine, as is a few friends or family members. It won't take a great deal of their time – 20 to 40-minutes at most – and you should ask them to treat it like a real presentation and act the way a real audience would act. While you don't necessarily need to record this practice session, you might want to just to see how you do in front of a live audience.

Your Secret Weapon

What are you really looking for in your recorded practice sessions? Firstly, you want to identify the "ahs" and "ums". Don't get too hung up on these. It just shows you as human. But you also don't want to have the "ahs" and "ums" totally distract from the message that you are sending. Videotaping yourself will help you identify those speech hang-ups and eliminate them. Remember silence is way better than a single "ah" or "um".

Videotaping the presentation will also help you eliminate some of the slow parts. These are the parts of the presentation when you may feel while watching it, as though it's just not making sense, or that it's not coming across the way that you want it to. Maybe you find a part of your presentation to be really slow or really dull. By reviewing the tape, you might get ideas about what you can do to spice it up. It's also going to identify the points that are to be changed or removed altogether because your presentation is 50-minutes long, and you need to get it down to 20-minutes.

On the other hand, it will also help you identify the areas that should be emphasized. If you find a really powerful point within the presentation, one that will ultimately sell these people on your products and services, you want to make sure it has a lot of emphasis. If it doesn't, videotaping will clearly show this, and you can make changes accordingly.

Benefits of Practicing

One of the biggest benefits of practicing is that you're going to be able to discover some awkward words or phrases. These could be words or phrases that sounded great when you were creating your presentation – but it may not sound so good when you say it out loud.

Practicing also gives you a chance to see if your personality is coming across the way you want it to. A lot of times it's easy for people to get their personality across. However, when they present in front of a group of people, they get nervous and their personality contracts. It doesn't come across the way that they want it to. One of the many benefits of practicing is that it will allow you to maximize your personality.

Practicing also gives you a chance to check your energy level. Maybe you're flushed, talking way too fast, and darting your eyes back and forth. That's too much energy. Or maybe your speech and tone are too slow and boring, hardly showing any energy at all. Maybe your energy level is perfect and you're talking and moving smoothly, clearly, and seem interesting. Videotaping yourself practicing will let you make sure your energy level is where you want it to be.

Watching your practice video will also give you a chance to check the timing of the presentation. Check to make sure that the presentation is within the 20 to 40-minute time frame, but also check the timing of the slides and the visual aids. You want to make sure that the timing of everything is working together to make the presentation better. If you notice any glitches, you'll be able to fix that via your practice sessions.

Ultimately, the biggest benefit you're going to get from videotaping your practice sessions is that it will build confidence and will get rid of some of your nerves. Remember that confidence is the key to all of this. When you practice enough, you'll know that you're getting your message across the way you want to. And that will let you give your presentation in the highest-quality manner.

Preparing for Your Presentation – Common Questions Answered

This section will answer the most common questions that people who follow this program have asked.

How should I dress?

It may seem funny or odd, but this is the first thing people often think about when preparing for their presentation, and while it's a valid concern, it's ultimately up to you. Business casual/professional attire, such as a suit with no tie, often works very well because it can be adapted to many different situations. It really does depend on your personality and your style. If you'll be talking to a room full of blue-collar managers of some type of business in your target market and they are dressed in their business uniforms and you come in a brand new flashy $1,500 suit, it could turn people off.

The flip side of it is if you sell high-end business-to-business (B2B) products and services, and everybody in your audience is going to be in really nice suits. You don't want to come in wearing jeans and a golf shirt because you're going to lose credibility. Just don't stress about it too much, don't go to an extreme either way, and you'll be fine.

Who orders the food?

Usually, the bank but this is definitely something you need to discuss with them. Most of the time the bank will help you out, even if it's through a 50-50 split. If you do end up splitting the cost, the bank typically handles the ordering as they know what restaurants are in the area, caterers they've used before, etc. Do make sure you work with the bank on this one, but usually they are the ones that take care of this.

How should the room be set up?

You may not have a lot of flexibility in their facility, because their meeting room may only be a certain size, and the way the projector's set up, etc. You may not be able to do too much. If you do have flexibility, you should try to set the room up in a U-shape. The reason for that is because everybody can see everybody else and all their eyes will be focused on you giving the presentation. But then you can also walk around and help individuals if they have questions. So a U-shape is the best scenario if you can do it.

Name tags or name tents?

Believe it or not this is a very common question, and the answer is that there is no right or wrong here. The only wrong thing to do is to not have either. You definitely need name tags or name tents because when you are meeting people you want to be able to call them by their first name and make the conversation seem more personable. Know that you should provide these items and that you should not depend on the bank or credit union to provide it.

Who provides notepads and pens?

You should have a single page fill-in-the-blank worksheet created for them to go through. You should come prepared with some pens for them to fill those out, and some notepads that will allow them to jot down extra notes. However, the bank will often be more than happy to provide these for your attendees, because they most likely all have their name, logo, and brand on it.

Who provides the projector/TV/monitor?

This one will be on the bank. The chances are good that they already have one that can hook up to any laptop and be able to go through a PowerPoint presentation. However, if they don't, you can rent one at any office supplies store. They are not very expensive, especially when you're just renting one for the day. But you absolutely want to use one because PowerPoint presentations are one of the most effective tools you have at your disposal. Of course, if you're really good at drawing things and want to use a whiteboard or a flip chart, that's fine too. Just make sure that the bank has those items available for you to use, too.

Should the bank contact attend?

You should insist that they do, especially the first one. Having them present will allow them to see the value of the presentation that you are giving. Invite them to sit in through the whole presentation. Most of them will anyway, especially when you first start working with them. But if you can get them to stay and see the value you're providing, it's going to make it easier for you to get referrals from them.

When is lunch served?

Of all the common questions, this might be the most common. It's ideal if you can work with the bank to have lunch delivered about 30-minutes after the presentation has begun. You can tell your attendees that lunch will arrive in a few minutes by saying something such as, **"I know everyone is ready for lunch. I spoke with Barb (your bank contact) and she said it would be delivered in about 30-minutes. In respect of everyone's time why don't we get started now. I should be done by the time the food arrives and then we can do Q&A while we're eating. Does that sound fair?"**

If you can manage to have the food delivered 30-minutes after you get started, you get everybody to focus on you and you don't have to worry about them eating and getting up to get their drinks or napkins and being a distraction to everyone in the room. Eating lunch during the Q&A can also be a more relaxing atmosphere, which works out perfectly because people will feel more comfortable asking questions.

But what if that doesn't work and they want to eat lunch during the presentation? Don't be worried about it too much. Try and have it delivered before you get started then let them start eating before you even begin. The one thing that you want to do is make sure that you've already eaten. You do not want to eat with them, you want to be able to spend your time making your presentation and answering questions.

When should I take questions?

This really depends on your presentation and your style. You can do it during the presentation, or you can wait until after. Whatever you decide, make sure that you set that expectation at the beginning. Either say, **"Just stop me if anything is unclear and I'll go over it,"** or say, **"I know there will be a lot of questions during the presentation but if we can hold them until the end, that will allow us to get through the presentation as quickly as possible. After that we'll have lots of time to answer any questions that you might have. Simply jot down any questions you have, and I'll be happy to go over them after the presentation."** If you do allow questions during the presentation, be careful not to take too long answering them. Taking too long throws everything else off, including your timing, and you don't want to do that. If you have a 30-minute presentation and you spend 10-minutes answering a single question you could see how that could really alienate the other attendees. It's for this reason that many choose to answer questions at the end of the presentation, to keep things tight and focused.

Even though expectations are set, some people will still ask questions throughout the presentation. Sometimes you'll be able to answer them quickly but if you can't, say, **"you know that's a great question. If you don't mind writing it down, I will answer it at the end of the presentation."** Nobody should have a problem with that.

Common Mistakes

The biggest mistake you could make during this portion of preparing for the presentation is forgetting to customize the presentation for a new audience. It would be quite embarrassing if you show the slide saying thanks to ABC bank, but the slide you have up is XYZ bank. So you want to make sure you take a few minutes and update it accordingly.

The other common mistake is not practicing as much as you should. You never want to think that you know the material so well that you don't need to practice. You want to invest the time in practicing the presentation and videotaping it and making sure that it's the message that you want to get across.

That leads right into the next common mistake - not recording your practice sessions. It cannot be stressed enough how important this is. Recording your practice on video is so revealing and so helpful; it's something that absolutely needs to be done.

But recording yourself isn't going to do much good if you don't review it and listen to it and neglecting to do so is another big mistake.

Repetition is a great mode of learning. This is going to help you get your message across so much more consistently and confidently.

What Not to Do

The first thing that you definitely don't want to do is to make your presentation so generic you don't have to customize it. You want to make everybody there feel like you created that presentation for them. So customize it as much as possible for each presentation that you have.

Next, don't avoid practice. Make sure that you're practicing and that you're trying to get at least 10 to 15 practice sessions in, and that you're videotaping at least 5 of them. Strip the audio off the best one and listen to it over and over again.

Lastly, don't assume the bank has everything covered. If you assume that they've got everything that they're going to need, it will likely come back to bite you. When you make this assumption, the smallest thing can turn into a huge ordeal all because you assumed someone else was taking care of it. You need to make sure that the expectations are set with the bank and that everyone knows what they need to cover and what their responsibilities are, so it runs as smoothly as possible.

Time for Action

Now you know what you need to do and it's time to customize your presentation for your first lunch-and-learn. Once you do, you can get your first practice session recorded within 24 hours.

Also, get familiar with the presentation checklist and add/remove things as needed. This will help guide you through that process and you can add things to it or remove things from it depending on what fits your personality and style.

Up Next

The next module is Step 5 - Confirm and Commit. You're going to learn how to confirm your lunch-and-learn presentations, which is very important. You must confirm because things sometimes change and you want to make sure that they still have you scheduled to make your presentation.

The next chapter will also focus on committing to these presentations mentally. This is important because you're a professional and it's important to commit to this presentation and not let any excuses cause you to avoid it.

Step Five - Confirm and Commit

In Step Five you'll learn how to properly confirm your appointment, and the importance of committing to it. This step is critical because you need to ensure that your lunch-and-learn is confirmed and that everyone is committed to it - not just the bank and the attendees, but you as well.

This step will give you a few call scripts to use when confirming with your bank contact. These are really easy to learn, straightforward, and anybody can use them. You'll also discover an email script you can send to bank contacts if, and only if, you can't get them on the phone.

Lastly, you'll also be given a checklist, which you can print off and use again and again that outlines the entire process and will make sure you stay on track and always have everything covered. Nothing will slip through the cracks with this checklist.

Why This is Important

There are three main reasons. Firstly, it helps manage expectations. The only way you can manage people is if the expectations are clearly set and outlined right at the beginning. Doing so will eliminate some of the surprises that may come up. Second, you'll also be able to go through the checklist, ensure that you have everything you need and that you've done everything right and in the right order up to this point. Lastly, confirming and committing also ensures professionalism. It shows that the presentation is still front and center in your mind, it shows your commitment, and it reinforces the professionalism that you have.

The Checklist

This checklist is a simple tool to keep you on track and organized. You can download an editable version in Microsoft Word as part of our CGP Toolkit (see the Tools and Resources section at the end of this book.)

For reference you can see the checklist below:

- ❑ Am I dressed appropriately for my audience?
- ❑ Who is ordering food?
    - ❑ Bank
    - ❑ Me
- ❑ When will food (and drinks) be delivered?
    - ❑ 30-minutes after we start
    - ❑ Before the L&L starts
- ❑ Room setup in U-shape
- ❑ Name tags/tents
- ❑ Pens
- ❑ Notepad
- ❑ "Fish Bowl" for attendee business cards
    - ❑ Ex., drawing for free 60-minute "*Your Topic* Audit"
- ❑ One-page Worksheet (front and/or back)
- ❑ Laptop with presentation
- ❑ Projector/TV/Monitor
    - ❑ Banks has one
    - ❑ I need to rent one
- ❑ Remote control for presentation (optional)
- ❑ Video Camera - you should record your presentations
    - ❑ Wireless lapel mic (optional)
- ❑ Digital Camera – have someone take a few pictures of you in action
- ❑ Flip-chart (optional)
- ❑ Extension cords
- ❑ Power strip

Confirmation Call Script

Before you even pick up the phone to confirm the date and time of your presentation, you need a confirmation call script. Remember that your confirmation call script doesn't have to be overly complicated. You already know that you've got the presentation, and your bank contact has already agreed to the presentation. This is just a straightforward phone call ensuring that everyone is still on the same page. Remember to use the checklist that you'll get later in this chapter and adapt it to your own style and needs as you see fit. This will help keep you on track and ensure you don't forget anything.

When you're on the phone with your bank contact, make sure that you confirm the number of attendees that will be there. You need to know in advance how many people will be there to give you an idea of how long the Q&A will be, how many handouts you need to bring, and to determine other logistics.

You also want to confirm the time, the lunch details, such as when it will arrive, and confirm who is ordering the lunch. Also remember to try and cover anything else you've talked about, especially if the bank contact has had concerns. Here is a simple confirmation call script that you can use along the way:

"Hello Mr/Mrs./Miss (person's name) this is (your name) calling to confirm the details about our lunch-and-learn on (the specific date at the specific time). Do you have a few minutes to make sure that we're on the same page and prepared for the lunch-and-learn?" (They'll say yes, and if they don't, just reschedule.)

Next, there is a big question that you must ask: that you get there about 60-minutes prior to the start of the presentation time. You want to make sure you can get set up, be there before the attendees arrive, and just ensure that you're comfortable with the room, the setup, and the equipment you'll be using.

"If it's okay with you, I'll arrive at" (blank time – approximately an hour before the meeting starts.) "Does that work for you?" After that you can launch into all of the things that you have discussed, as well as what's on your checklist.

"As previously discussed, we agreed who is ordering lunch, when will it be delivered, and that the projector will be there."

To end the phone call, simply thank them for all their help and reiterate how excited you are to bring value to their customers. You cannot emphasize this point enough, because this is the benefit the bank is directly receiving.

It's also important to reiterate this because some time may have passed since you initially scheduled the lunch-and-learn, and their excitement may have faded a bit. Reminding them about the value they're bringing their customers will reignite that spark and get them excited about the idea again.

End with a simple, "I look forward to seeing you on (whatever day and time that is.)"

So that's your script if you've reached them on the phone. But what if you get voicemail?

Voicemail Script

Here is a very simple voicemail script.

"Hello Mr/Mrs./Miss (their name), this is (your name) calling to confirm the details about our lunch-and-learn on (specific date at specific time). I will send you an email outlining all the details. Please review and let me know if you have any changes or questions.

You can always call me at (your phone number) if you would like to talk live.

Thanks for your time and I'll get that email sent off right now."

The reason this script is so valuable is because it allows you to give them your information, let them know why you're calling and also give them a heads up that an email is coming.

You can change these as you need to, but they are simple and straightforward for a reason – because your bank contact is busy and doesn't have time to be on the phone or buried in their email all day. Remember to keep these very short and simple.

Remember to always follow up with a phone call the day before the lunch-and-learn, at minimum. If you just made the appointment two weeks ago, it's probably fine to wait until a day or two before the lunch-and-learn. But if you scheduled it 60-days ago, you may want to call a full week or two in advance. This will remind them of the presentation and will give you lots of time in advance if they happen to have forgotten about it and need to reschedule.

Confirmation Email Swipe File

If you need to send them an email with the details, it can be helpful to have a confirmation email script to follow as well. Use email only if you don't talk to your contact live. If you end up leaving a voicemail or a message with the gatekeeper, then send the email but never send an email without first trying a phone call. This is the most professional way to do it and gives them a heads up that you're trying to reach them before they get an email from you.

Your email will need to cover all the details that were covered in the call script so make sure you use the same checklist, checking off items that have been discussed.

The email script is very similar to the call script, with the exception that you'll need to mention the call you've already made to them.

"Hello Mr/Mrs./Miss (their name), I left a voicemail for you this morning regarding our upcoming lunch-and-learn on (specific date at specific time). Do you have a few minutes to review the details and let me know if everything looks okay to you? If it's okay with you I will arrive at (specific time) to get the room set up and conduct a quick test run.

As previously discussed, we agreed on (list those items out).

Thanks for your help Mr./Mrs./Miss (name). I'm real excited to give a ton of value to your customers. I look forward to seeing you on (specific date). In the meantime, please feel free to contact me if you have any changes or questions.

I will contact you by phone on [time and date] to confirm again. Unless of course, you respond to this email letting me know we're good to go."

Your Commitment

It is so important that you remain fully committed to this, and any, lunch-and-learn that you schedule and that you don't let anything get in the way of you presenting.

This is simply a matter of professionalism, and if you want to maintain it, you need to be committed and show that commitment to everyone involved in the lunch-and-learn.

While it may sound easy and obvious, it's not so for people who get sidetracked and loses sight of the end goal – to present the lunch-and-learn, get more clients, and make more money!

Life will always happen, but make sure that you're sticking to your commitments and remaining excited about these lunch-and-learns so that you can enjoy all the other life moments even more!

Remember that once a bank contact gives you the opportunity to walk through the door, they may not do it again so seize the moment!

The chances are good that if you've reached this point in the book, you are already committed and dedicate., You're already ahead of the game in separating yourself from the rest of the pack. Well done!

Common Mistakes to Avoid

Confirming the date and time of your presentation may seem like a no-brainer, but it's shocking how many people make the rookie mistake of not doing so. They choose not to confirm because they assume that everything is already taken care of. You do not want to be that person. You always want to confirm because it shows professionalism and shows your dedication and commitment.

Doing a super quick confirmation, which is something like, "I'm calling to make sure we're still on for tomorrow. We are great. Okay, bye," also doesn't count for much. Because in addition to not calling at all, neglecting to mention any of the other details is a big mistake. This is why you need to have your checklist when you call, to make sure all the details are covered for both of you.

The other common mistake is to not be committed to the lunch-and-learn. While things may come up that prevent you from being there, unless it's an emergency you need to try your best to remain professional and always, always honor your commitments.

What Not to Do

In addition to these common mistakes, what should you *not* do? Firstly, don't send an email confirmation only. Don't just send an email and assume that they got it and that everything is okay. You have got to make a phone call first, and then only send an email if you don't speak with your contact on the phone.

Don't ignore the checklist. It will help guide you and keeps you focused on what you need to do.

And lastly, but certainly not least, don't let excuses prevent you from fully committing to your lunch-and-learn.

Time for Action

Now you're ready to confirm your lunch-and-learn! If you have one scheduled, use the call scripts to confirm it, tweaking it as needed. It should fit your style and your personality. But call first, send an email if you get voicemail, and make sure that you tell them that an email is coming their way. Do all of this while using your checklist.

Action item number two is to commit yourself to your lunch-and-learn. Commit to it, eliminate obstacles and excuses, free your mind and get ready to give them a hell of a lunch-and-learn.

Up Next

The next module is Step 6, which will help you conduct your lunch-and-learn and convey your message in an effective way. You're also going to learn a simple no pressure way to generate clients, which is the fun part and why you're doing L&L's in the first place!

Step Six - Convey Your Message and Close Deals

Step six is all about conveying your message and "closing deals" – might be more appropriately called "next actions". There are three next possible actions, and they all use no-pressure methods.

What You'll Learn

In this step, you'll learn the different guidelines you can follow to deliver a powerful message. You'll also learn not only how to get clients, but how to get them to come to you – all using no pressure methods. This is important because you want to bring as much value to your audience as possible.

When you use these tips and techniques to do that, you'll be able to add that value to these presentations and make them enjoyable for your audience. And of course, you want to get more clients – that's the ultimate goal. This step will teach you how to do that.

Conveying Your Message

When conveying your message, the first thing you need to remember is that it's not about you, it's about them. It's crucial to remember that, because you're building this presentation with the intention of helping your attendees, not just talking about yourself or your company.

Keep the focus on them and resist the urge to talk about how great you are. You need to tell them your credentials, but you don't need to go on and on about it. You mainly need to talk about a problem they're having and give them the solution to that problem.

You know how to prepare and present a great lunch-and-learn, and now is the time that you're going to be able to convey your message. You'll be able to execute everything that you've practiced. And, using these top ten tips, you'll be able to do it flawlessly.

Keep your intro short

Again, please remember, it's not about you it's about them. While you do need to introduce yourself and build a little bit of credibility, you still want to do it in a very short and concise manner.

Tell stories

Whenever possible use a story or a case study to prove your point. The mind processes information better when told in story form. Do that as often as possible.

Keep it relevant to your message

You don't want to be talking about too many things at once. If you do, many of those things will be irrelevant and will just cause confusion.

Customize it

Each and every lunch-and-learn is going to be a little bit different so you want to make sure that you customize it to the audience that you're presenting it to.

Keep it simple

You don't want to overcomplicate things and possibly lose your audience during the presentation. You want to keep it simple, have a few main points, and make sure that they are explained in a way that is easy to understand.

Have a one-pager

A one-page fill-in-the-blank worksheet is really powerful and it's proven to increase the retention and attention of the audience.

Never read your slides

There is one exception here, and that's if you're reading a quote or fact. Otherwise, you never want to read your slides. That's a surefire way to make a presentation that's excruciatingly boring for you and your audience.

However, if you're reading a quote or a fact that is provided by a third party, you want to make sure that you do read that as-is so there's no confusion.

Skip jargons and acronyms

Sometimes this is very difficult to do but try to avoid jargons and acronyms when you can. This is important because you don't want to assume that your audience knows everything that you do. When you use industry acronyms that they don't understand, a lot of times they won't ask what you mean because they feel as though they should know (although that's not necessarily the case.) Try and skip any jargon or acronyms if at all possible, and everyone will be on the same page throughout the entire presentation.

Focus on the audience

This tip may be a bit obvious, but you really have to make sure you're focusing on the audience and that you're not distracted by anything else. Make sure that the blinds are drawn in the room, so all the focus in the room is on you.

Always do Q&A

At some point you need to do Q&A, even if there is only a little bit of time remaining. You need to give the audience the opportunity to ask questions. A lot of times what happens is, nobody will ask that first question because they don't feel completely comfortable doing so. Because of this it's a good idea to have a few common questions available you can review, and get it started. By saying things like, "I get asked all the time..." or "One of the most common questions I get...." This will build the confidence and the comfort level in the room and will make them feel better about asking you questions.

Closing Deals aka Next Actions

Concluding the presentation is the time to convert prospects into clients and take those next actions.

The first thing you want to do during this time is give your attendees a valuable giveaway. Whether it's a printed book, printed report, a CD, DVD, whatever you want to give them as that valuable giveaway.

Remember, we can help you with creating those giveaways. Contact us at our other site: CredibilityBook.com.

Drawing for a contest winner can also be a very successful next action step. This can be a gift card, a discount on your services, anything that you think will be valuable to them. Of course, if you've had them put their business cards in a fish bowl or hat, you're the real winner because you now have all of their contact information.

You can also conclude your presentation with something like, "If you've found this information useful and would like to discuss it further please see me after and we can schedule a time to meet and see if this is a good fit for you." This is a low-key way to get them to come to you. The chances are good that they did find the information useful, and many of them would like to discuss it further. Instead of chasing after them, you're inviting them to come to you.

Now you're ready to actually get clients, and this will come very naturally after providing them with a presentation that's of high value to them, giving them a valuable giveaway, and you offering to sit down and talk to them with no obligation. The attendees that resonated with your presentation will come up to you with their question, or to speak further about certain points.

Whatever you do, don't use high-pressure sales tactics. If you're talking to somebody and they have questions but they're not ready to commit to meeting with you outside of this presentation environment, you have every right to ask them to sit down and chat to see if it will be a good fit. If they aren't interested, that's okay - it's won't be right for everybody.

You just want to be transparent as possible, while being confident but not pushy. It's all about getting to the next action step.

Sometimes customers may hire you depending on the services that you provide. It may be a one-call close in which there's not a lot of additional content. It's rare, but it can happen. This shouldn't be your main focus, because your main focus really, is to handle the people that want additional information.

Selling is Communicating and Educating

While not a major part of this course, sales skills are important and do need to be mentioned. You may already be experienced in sales and ahead of the game, but there are a few things that you should be aware of.

The first is think of selling more like communication skills versus sales skills. It's a better way to look at it - communicating with a perspective buyer of your products or services. You want to be able to communicate with them in an upfront, honest, transparent way.

There are methods of how to communicate in a no-pressure way. At Salestrainingweekly.com you can get some free lessons. Just logon and get some free sales training. If it's a good fit for you, you can then sign up to receive even more training sessions.

Sales skills are very important but again, it's more about the way that you communicate when you're met with objections. Sales is about making sure that what you're selling is a good fit for your customer.

It's knowing that your product is actually going to help them and tearing down the walls that buyers can sometimes put up.

Common Mistakes to Avoid

There are many common mistakes to be made, but one of the biggest is converting back to traditional marketing tactics and making it all about you. Instead, you need to focus on solving the attendees' problem.

Another common mistake is using high pressure sales methods. High pressure tactics will not work in a lunch-and-learn situation, so you should avoid them.

Another common mistake is being reluctant to improve on your presentation or your selling skills. When you convey your message and it doesn't go exactly how you hoped reviewing it and improving it is okay.

If needed to work on your selling skills; read books, attend trainings, do whatever you can to improve. Because when you are able to communicate effectively in a sales environment it's going to help you earn more income and that's really what it's all about.

What Not to Do

Don't try to be someone you're not. A lot of times when people get in front of a group to give a presentation, they turn into somebody that they're not.

Either they try to be funny, or they try and be super professional rather than trying to show their personality. The bottom line is, be yourself.

Don't stress about the outcome too much. It's good to have goals, but don't stress over an outcome you can't control.

You can only control your presentation and how you present it. Don't stress over anything else.

Also, don't put a lot of pressure on people. It comes across as desperate, and you don't want that.

Time for Action

Congrats! You've completed Step 6. There are a couple of action steps that will help you keep the momentum going.

Continue to practice your presentation until your lunch-and-learn. Keep practicing going over the steps of recording yourself, tweaking it as needed, and improving it as needed.

Another action item is to visualize what you want and make it happen. This is what it's all about. Visualize your presentation. Visualize people coming up to you after the presentation wanting more information.

It's amazing when you execute that plan and execute your visualization and it all plays out exactly the same way.

It will happen more often than you think.

Up Next

Up next is Step 7, where you'll learn how to convert your presentation into a webinar. Be aware that this isn't going to be for everybody, but it will cover why you should use webinars and how they're a good supplement to your live lunch-and-learns. Step 7 also talks about whether to use automated webinars or actual live webinars, and what services you might want to use.

Step Seven - Convert to a Webinar

Webinars can be a very lucrative way to generate leads and convert leads into customers. In this step you'll learn how to convert your in-person L&L into an online webinar.

IMPORTANT: this chapter can be an entire training by itself. In fact, I help many students create webinar funnels for many different purposes. With that in mind and given the scope of this book we will not cover every tiny detail of webinars. However, we will cover them enough, so you can use them effectively as a compliment to your live L&L's.

Quick Recap

Before we get started with this chapter let's look back at everything, we've learned so far:

☑ In step one you need to construct your lists.

☑ The second step is to contact all of the people on your list - the bank contacts.

☑ In the third step your presentation was actually created.

☑ In Step 4 you learned how to customize, practice and prepare your presentation. The most important part of Step 4 is to practice by recording your presentations and then listening to the best one over and over getting it down so that you know exactly what you're going to say.

☑ In Step 5 you learned how to confirm and commit. You want to always make sure that you're confirming and that everything is taken care of. And then of course you need to commit not only to the bank contact, but to yourself. You're a professional, and you need to make sure that you commit to what you say you'll do.

☑ In Step 6 you learned how to convey your message, close deals and give the attendees their next actions.

Now you've arrived at Step 7, which is, Convert to Webinars. Quite frankly, using webinars isn't right for everybody, but it is a supplement to your live lunch-and-learns, and it is a very effective one.

Why Webinars

At some point, you may want to convert to or complement your live lunch-and-learn with webinars. Webinars are a very powerful tool and for some it makes sense to use that tool in their business. This section is important so that you know for sure whether it's going to be a good fit for you.

In Step 7 you'll learn are a few different things. First of all, what benefits webinars bring, as well as some of the weaknesses that are inherent to them.

You'll also learn about automated webinars versus live webinars.

You'll also learn how there are many webinar services out there, and some are way more expensive than others. Here you'll learn which ones are the best, and why you might not have to pay top dollar for them.

All of this is important because you need to understand how webinars work, so you can make an educated decision for your business. You also need to understand the options available to you.

Webinar Defined

Let's first define what a webinar is. Google defines it as, "a seminar conducted over the Internet." That's pretty simple and straight forward, and that's really all it is.

Webinar Strengths

Firstly, it saves time because you can do it from your home or office or wherever. You don't have to leave, and that leads into saving money because you can just stay at the office and there is no travel or extra expenses involved.

Webinars are also very flexible. You can test different slides and message and get real time feedback.

You can also get a lot more people to attend a webinar than an in-person L&L. Usually the room will only hold 16-20 people for a live presentation. A webinar you can get as many as 1,000 or more to attend at one time.

It's also convenient for attendees because some attendees will prefer to do webinars where they are able to log on and watch it from their computer.

Webinar Weaknesses

These strengths are also some of the weakness of webinars. Because no one is attending in person, it is not as personal as in-person lunch-and-learns. When in doubt, always choose the live lunch-and-learns over webinars because there's nothing more impactful than being in front of somebody in a live setting. Sometimes that can't happen, and so webinars are a good alternative or a good complement to the live lunch-and-learns. Anything live and in person is going to be much better.

The potential for talking about next actions in webinars are also not as high as an in-person lunch-and-learns. With webinars, really the best you can do is simply present a question to the group, because you can't narrow it down to a one and one conversation with somebody. Those conversations for next actions have to take place at another time and that makes it somewhat more difficult as well.

Webinars tend to lead to relationships that are not as strong as they are when you're in front of somebody. Now that's not to say that you can't build good relationships or credibility via a webinar, because you can, it's just not as powerful as if it was face-to-face.

Also know that with webinars, you're likely going to be the one that has to bring in the attendees. Some banks will be open to inviting their customers to a webinar, but that usually doesn't happen until you have some sort of relationship with the bank. That's something to consider as well.

And then, while some attendees like to stay in their office and watch a webinar, others like to get out of the office and get a free lunch and discover something valuable that's going to help their business.

How to Use Webinars

Ideally, you're using webinars as a supplement to your live L&L's and not a replacement. At least not at the beginning.

The reason for that is because you want to get a flood of clients quickly. And the best way to do that is with a live L&L and not a webinar. That doesn't mean you can't use webinars from the start. I'm just here to tell you when you do live L&L's to get your client generation flowing it works better.

As you begin to start implementing webinars into your marketing a great option is when you want to introduce new products or services.

For example, you give a lunch-and-learn on a specific topic at a bank. Then as a follow-up you offer those attendees the opportunity to attend your webinar on a new topic. They already know you, trust you and view you as the go-to expert. The likelihood of them attending the webinar will be very high.

Webinars are very flexible, and these are just a couple of examples. But hopefully these examples will get you started using webinars at some level in your business.

When to Use Webinars

The best time to use webinars are as a follow-up to your live, in-person presentations.

Please start with live lunch-and-learns. These are going to have the biggest impact and will provide you with the most clients in the fastest possible way; doing this will give you the best start. It's a proven process so don't try and reinvent the wheel. Just follow the system and use the system, and then use webinars as a complementary tool versus a replacement to your live lunch-and-learns.

Automated vs Live Webinars

Automated webinars are something that you can record as a video, or as an actual live webinar. They can play automatically so you don't have to be there for them. This can be beneficial because you don't have to spend a lot of time doing webinars; you can just have them running and it will still do the same job it would as if you were there doing it live.

Both automated and live webinars should be a part of your webinar arsenal; it's always important to use both. Because if you were to draw a chart that went from top to bottom, the top being the best, it would be live lunch-and-learns. Then the second would be live webinars and the third would be automated webinars.

An automated webinar makes it easier to get your message out there because you record it once and then replay it over and over. Automated webinars can be watched when somebody signs up, or they can choose a certain time that you have predetermined.

A great way to create an automated webinar is by recording a live webinar and then using that as your automated one. That's going to give it more of a live feel, even though it is recorded. That will also allow you to focus on quality content, and most attendees won't care if it's recorded or not as long as the content is good.

For best results, live webinars are the best way to go because it's in real time. They are more authentic and, some attendees just want to know it's live.

Does it really matter if it's live or not? Not really. But live webinars do lead to better conversions. You can have them go to a website that's right there, so if the product is only available for 72 hours, it gives them a better chance of actually getting it. You can also lose credibility if you say, "only for 72 hours" in an automated webinar and that same presentation is up a month later and the offer is still available well past the 72-hour mark.

What Presentation to Use on Your Webinar

There are a lot of different things that you can do but try the same one you are using as your live lunch-and-learn first. If you're using it as a complement to introduce a new product, then it is going to be a little bit different and remember, you can go much longer on webinars than you can in a live lunch-and-learn.

Typical webinars are anywhere from 60 to 120-minutes. Some may go longer, although those are more of a workshop than just a webinar. Try to stick to the 60 to 90-minute mark because after that it gets pretty exhausting. It's also proven that 20-minutes is about the length of time that people can really hold their attention fully. When you go beyond that it starts to get difficult.

Webinar Services

In our world of fast-moving technology that seems to change by the minute the below recommendations may have changed. To get the most up-to-date list of tools and resources please see the "Tools and Resources" section in the back of this book.

There are many automated webinar services that you can use. One that is highly recommended is StealthSeminar.com. They have a ton of different services and different features that you can use and it's relatively inexpensive.

A key feature you get with StealthSeminar is their Just-in-Time (JIT) function. This makes it appear that the visitor got there "just-in-time" for the next webinar. Regardless of when they arrive on the page the next webinar appears to be starting in a matter of minutes. This feature has been proven to improve conversions. Many other providers have copied this feature.

Another top-quality provider is EverWebinar. There system is very easy-to-use and very cost efficient.

As far as live webinars go, there are two very popular services.

The most popular service is GoToWebinar. The positive for GTW is that they are by far the industry leader. Everybody and their mother uses them. It's a quality service that's very reliable. Be prepared however, they are very, very expensive. Ridiculously so in my opinion.

A great alternative to GTW, and what I personally use, is Zoom.com. They provide a great service at a reasonable cost. You can run test webinars with a handful of people and see how you like it.

Another great alternative is EasyWebinar.com. It is also very flexible and offers automated webinars.

Common Mistakes to Avoid

There are a few common mistakes when it comes to using webinars for lunch-and-learns. The biggest one is starting with webinars before doing in person lunch-and-learns. Make sure you present in person lunch-and-learns first, before you venture into webinars. It's just proven to be a better way to do things.

Once you start your webinars, packing too much into it is another common mistake. It's easy to visualize doing a live lunch-and-learn and making the content piece of it only 20 to 30 minutes. You can do that because you have live people there.

They know it's over lunch, they know they're not going to be there for much more than 60-minutes, and so you need to be able to condense your content into that time frame. But in a webinar, you can visualize yourself having more freedom to expand on each and every topic, each and every aspect of your presentation.

You want to really resist that temptation and continue to keep the focus on them and the one problem one solution scenario.

The last common mistake is using only automated or only live webinars. There should be a mixture, so you can get the best of both worlds.

You can have most of your content running via automated webinars but every now and then, run a live webinar on a new topic or a new solution.

Time for Action

It needs to be stressed that you should only test the water with webinars after you have done a handful of live, in person lunch-and-learns.

When you're ready to start testing and implementing webinars, conduct a live webinar first, even if there are just a few people in attendance. Run it live first and record it.

You can then use that recording for your automated webinar. It will make the automated webinar sound and appear live and more authentic because it was recorded live.

If you're not happy with the first live one, then do another live one and keep doing them until you nail it. Always record them so when you do conduct one, you're happy with it and you can use that as your automated webinar.

Up Next

Congratulations! You're done with this book and training system. The only thing left for you to do is to implement it and start generating clients!

Be sure to "rinse and repeat" this process as often as you need. It works, if you work it.

Once you do a lunch-and-learn make sure you do more lunch-and-learns. That's the type of activity that is going to bring in the clients, the easiest, fastest way possible.

Then, when your funnel is so full that you can't even do lunch-and-learns anymore because you have so much business – raise your prices!

You now have The Client Getting P.L.A.N. - a proven system you can follow step-by-step. You can use it any time you want, and you can use it over and over again whenever you need to get more clients.

While this book is done, your journey has just begun. Keep in touch and share your successes, share your insight. If you have ideas or suggestions of how to improve this system, please share them with me because I really want to hear them. Please feel free to contact me directly at: support@clientgettingplan.com.

Quick Tips to Maximize the P.L.A.N.

Do you want to really blow people away during your lunch-and-learn presentations? I mean really take it to the next level and separate yourself for everyone else out there that you're competing with? Do these three simple things:

1. Don't use business cards. Bring them, but don't rely on them. *Instead use printed books, CDs, DVDs and free reports with your information contained inside.* Have a business card attached if you must but using a card alone certainly won't distinguish you from the pack. You need to do something different than the rest. Something that says you go that extra mile every single time. We can help you with this. Visit our site for all the details: CredibilityBook.com

2. Remember to keep it short. When preparing your presentation make sure it's no longer than 20 to 40-minutes. Yes, you may have the room booked for a full hour or more, but you shouldn't be the one doing all the talking for that entire time. You need to give the guests time to ask questions, and time for you to address their specific needs.

3. Make sure you work the room. No one wants to attend a presentation where one person stands at the front of the room and just speaks the entire time, without any interaction. It's ineffective, and no one will want to come back to another presentation. Instead, work the room. Shake hands, kiss babies, give small waves and nods, and point people out when certain topics seem to resonate with them. It's okay to be somewhat casual and informal here, because you're only there to help!

Want Help Putting the P.L.A.N. Into Action?

Want to know how to get started fast?

That's easy, do the first step! Make your lists of topics and your bank contact list. You'll never achieve your goals, desires and dreams if you don't take action.

Getting started creates momentum. And once momentum has been created you can use it to get in an "action state" and just keep it rolling.

Two "Action Helper" Options

Books are great. I think we can all agree on that. But sometimes, depending on how you learn, you may want additional help to get things rolling.

There are two ways you can enhance your learning and implement the Client Getting PLAN as quickly as possible:

1. Join our full online training course with videos, audios, templates, swipes, etc. This training course also comes with a private support where you can post questions. To see all the details go to:

   http://clientgettingplan.com/course

2. Apply for my mentoring program. I take on a handful of clients every few months to help them with not only implementing this client generating system but with pretty much everything else in their business. Including; marketing, establishing credibility, increasing conversions, building passive income

profit centers – in other words creating income streams that they create once but get paid for over and over again, plus much more. If you'd like a no obligation 30-minute free coaching session you can schedule it here:

http://clientgettingplan.com/schedule

Closing Thoughts

The Client Getting P.L.A.N. really is a powerful way to generate all the clients you can handle. It's easy-to-do and can be a blast.

You'll be providing a great service to your clients as well as the bank or whatever business or association you use to deliver your L&Ls.

Providing value, education and helping your target market is the best way to sell. In fact, it's not really selling is it? How awesome is that?

The PLAN works IF you work it... So go work it!

About the Author

Drew Laughlin is widely considered to be one of the top marketing consultants, trainers and product creators for entrepreneurs, consultants and professional service businesses.

He has helped thousands of businesses and solo- practitioners create businesses that are not only profitable but one's they love. Drew's clients spend less time working in their business and more time with their families and doing the things they love. While at the same time making more money.

Drew's home base in Omaha, NE and he spends as much time as possible with his wife and two children doing the things they love; Husker games, golfing, skiing, going to the lake and hanging with friends on the beach (not in Omaha!).

You can learn more about Drew here:

ClientGettingPlan.com/about

Want the Ultimate Marketing Asset for Your Business?

Have you ever wanted a real-life print book with your name on it?

I bet your answer is, "Of course I do!"

Even in today's digital world nothing replaces a print book when it comes to positioning yourself as an authority in your marketplace.

And it's easier than ever before to get your book published, fast. But it can get confusing and intimidating if you don't know the publishing landscape.

We want to help answer any questions you might have by offering you the free one-pager and walk-thru video that shows you why a Credibility Book is the easiest, quickest and best way for you to build instant authority in your marketplace… and how you can get your own in 45-days or less!

Go here for instant access:

CredibilityBook.com

Tools and Resources

Due to the ever changing technology world that we live in I thought it would be best to include ALL of the recommended tools and resources that you will need on a webpage instead of listing them here.

If a resource changes or goes away it is easy to update a webpage. A book? Not-so-much. It makes sense, right?

This way you'll know with 100% confidence that you are getting the latest and greatest list of tools and resources you should be using in your business.

To get this complete list go to:

http://clientgettingplan.com/resources

CGP TOOLKIT

Throughout this book we referenced the *CGP Toolkit*. This is a collection of templates, worksheets, swipe files, etc. In short, this toolkit contains everything you need to get started quickly and easier than doing everything from scratch.

Since you own this book you can get this toolkit at a special price at the link below:

http://clientgettingplan.com/toolkit